W9-CCL-542

Not Book Club Material

Aaron Zevy

TUMBLEWEED PRESS, INC.

Copyright © Tumbleweed Press 2021. All rights reserved.

Not Book Club Material

Aaron Zevy

Copyright © Tumbleweed Press 2021. All rights reserved.

This book is a work of both imagination and lived experiences mixed together to delight and entertain. In some cases I have tried to recreate certain events, locales and conversations from my memories of them... and then I embellish as is my way. In order to maintain their anonymity in some instances I have changed the names of individuals and places, and I may have changed what happened or did not. Do not assume anything in this book is true or accurate. Do not assume that any of the individuals in the book are real, living or dead. Enjoy.

No part of this book may be reproduced, or stored in a retrieval system, or transmitted in any form or by any means, electronic, mechanical, photocopying, recording, or otherwise, without express written permission of the publisher.

Edited by Jules Lewis
Copy edit by Miles Dorfman, Marianne Last, Faye Goldman
Cover design by Tatiana Sayig
Cover photo by Tatiana Sayig
Book design by Helen Prancic
Photographs courtesy of Darren Tunnicliff, Orly, and the Zevy family
Stock photographs: 123rf.com, Alamy, Getty Images, iStock, NASA, Pixabay, Unsplash
ISBN: 9798596940893

CONTENTS

THE BOOK CLUB

Photograph © SolStock / iStock

Before my first collection came out, I toyed with the notion of adding a recipe section in the middle of the book because many of the stories were about the Egyptian Jewish food I was raised on. Books, especially self-published story collections by completely unknown former powder paint salesmen are, as it turns out, surprisingly hard to market and I thought the recipes might be a compelling hook. One July morning, over a breakfast of scrambled eggs at the cottage, I made the mistake of casually suggesting it might be of interest for book clubs. I actually thought it was a pretty good idea. This led my sister-in-law to utter the sentence which became the family's favorite line in the summer of 2020.

"Your book," she said in her completely honest and unfiltered style, "is not book club material."

Before I could even react, my niece Danna came running out of the bedroom where she had, I was pretty sure, been fast asleep and added "Book clubs Uncle Ronnie? Seriously?"

I'm not going to lie. It kinda stung. They must have seen the look on my face and began a group backpedal befitting a team of circus unicyclists. Book clubs, they explained, read thick best-selling novels with complicated themes, motifs, and plotlines. Grey matter material they could discuss over coffee and low-fat gluten-free banana muffins. They went on to list a bunch of books as examples. Most of them appeared to have the word Crawdad in the title. Anyway, book clubs, they stated emphatically, did not read short story collections.

This, I knew, was patently untrue. Book clubs did, occasionally, include short story collections and humorous memoirs in their reading lists.

But that wasn't the point. I was just wondering if I should include a few pages of recipes like my mother's sofrito chicken. It was just an idea.

'Not book club material' became a bit of a catch all phrase that summer. We would apply it to a poorly executed dive off the dock, a bad pickle ball serve, and even a batch of BBQ chicken which had, because left on the grill a bit too long, dried up a little. It's good, but it's not book club material, someone would say with a smile. Teasing is part of the culture up at the cottage and Caroline and I are generally the prime targets. The irony of course is that in this instance I was pretty sure we were making fun of her when in fact, they were making fun of me.

That is only to say I could not hide my pleasure when, on Labour Day weekend, I received an email from Beth Middleton of the SVVGBC. The SVVGBC, for those of you who are not au courant with your California book club acronyms, is the Simi Valley Valley Girls Book Club. Beth Middleton was the Secretary-Treasurer. Or maybe she was the Treasurer-Secretary. I'm not entirely sure. I think she was in charge of collecting the fees so they could buy coffee and low-fat gluten free banana muffins. The members of the SVVGBC were not actually from Simi Valley, they all lived in nearby Moorpark, and they were not girls, from the valley or otherwise - they were empty nesters who, in addition to playing tennis, bridge, and speed walking, got together once a month to talk about books and gossip about the goings on in their town. Also, as I soon learned, their drink of choice was mojitos and their muffins were, as Beth Middleton liked to say with a giggle, full fucking fat.

Every month a member of the group would pick a book and when it was member Adele Ben-Simon's turn, she picked *Almost the Truth: Stories and Lies*, which was my book, because a cousin of hers, who I think was a third cousin of mine, had suggested she read it because like me, Adele was a child of Egyptian Jews.

So that's what she picked and there may have been a little grumbling, Beth Middleton dropped a few hints, by some of the more traditional and conservative members of the SVVGBC because the book was a thin collection of short humorous vignettes and not a thick sweeping historical saga replete with overriding themes about the human condition. Also, it did not have Crawdads in the title. Beth Middleton said it would be good to have a break from serious reading.

So the SVVGBC had read my book and Beth Middleton emailed me to ask if I would do a Zoom reading. Adele was going to make her sambozas. I think she meant to say sambousek, a delicious pastry filled either with cheese or ground meat and pomegranates, which was an appetizer staple in the Middle East, but she might have mixed it up with the Indian curry puff known as samosa.

Either way they were all very excited and I said I would be delighted.

I walked down the path to the dock where my family was congregated in order to announce that a book club in California had asked me to be a guest speaker. I auditioned a few zingers in my head and finally settled on "Not book club material eh? Well suck on that bitches!" Which, I admit, was not one which would have made Oscar Wilde green with envy "Damn, why didn't I think of that," but it was the best I could come up with. I mean, the walk to the dock was not that long and I was moving at a pretty good clip. But then I changed my mind. Not because I realized I was being petty, childish, immature, and small minded. But because, if I waited a little longer to tell them, I could be even more petty, childish, immature, and small minded.

And so, I did the Zoom reading. I spent a little more time than I care to admit choosing an outfit. I also got Danna to cut my hair, without telling her why, and spent the extra time required to trim my nose hairs. The reading went great. I read *Crossing the Nile*, which was a story about food and being a little different, and then, without needing much encouragement, read a second story, *Yorkdale*, the I hoped funny tale recounting the trip I took to the mall with my wheelchair bound friend Harold in order to buy him a mattress. It got a lot of laughs. There was then a short Q and A; I grandly espoused my thoughts about meta fiction. For a few short-lived (I am told I use 'ephemeral' too much) moments, I felt like a real writer. They toasted the book with a couple of rounds of mojitos, and then we all signed off. It was a great night.

It should have been a triumph but, I don't know why, it felt a little hollow. It was, as best as I could tell, the only book club that had ever taken on any of my books and it was beginning to look very much like the confirmation of the old adage, one which I still don't really understand, of the exception proving the rule. Not really book club material. So I never said anything. I only told Allie. Whatever revenge I was hoping to exact would, at best, be served at room temperature.

The reading occurred in September and with a blink of an eye, fall turned into winter and we conducted our annual Secret Santa, although using the Hebraic 'Hanukkah Harry' moniker, on Zoom. My bubble expanded to ten and, forgoing my annual migration to Florida, I saw the cottage for the first time under a blanket of ice and snow. We took turns making big dinners and then took hours picking the evening movie. I tried snowshoeing and, like most activities in my life, enjoyed talking about it better than actually doing it. There was no confusion about who was being made fun of when my brother later announced that in the middle of the hike, one I had badly overdressed for despite his protestations, I had turned to him and asked if he maybe had a towel so I could wipe my back clean of the accumulated sweat. I didn't go snowshoeing again. I confirmed I could not build a fire beyond burning up every section of the Sunday New York Times. I also confirmed that the secret to life was to spend the better part of 60 years lowering the bar as much as possible so that one day when you inexplicably and uncharacteristically decide to participate in the midnight tequila shot and toboggan run, your youngest niece Rena will gleefully proclaim it have to been epic.

I wrote stories almost every day that month of December. Some of the stories you are about to read. I wrote them on my iPhone, reclining on the couch facing the fire I had not built. I sent them to Kubes, and to Rob, and Ellen, and Mutley, and my cousin Morris, to Marianne, Miles, Jules and Tatiana, to Julie and Joel, to my brother-in-law Jamie and my sister Danielle in Israel, to Brian, to Elan and Malka, to Carainn and Karen, to Allan, my fellow Egyptian, to Elena, to Faye and to Steve and Fern, to Harold and Gili, who in turn forwarded them to their children, to Tuddy in Ottawa, and to other friends and family. I read them out loud ad nauseam at breakfast, lunch, and dinner, to my brother Dov, and to my sister-in-law Caroline, to Sammy, Danna, Rachel and Rena and their respective husbands and boyfriends. They all interrupted their school, jobs, life, family, TV, Instagram, and books to read and listen and, without exception, encourage.

I'm not sure if these stories are book club material. I'm not sure I care. But it turns out I was part of a pretty good book club all the same. Once in a while, one of the members will even drop off some muffins.

HOME MADE CAKE

My mother grew up in a large apartment on Rue Ismail Pasha in the Cairo suburb of Heliopolis. Some time after the 1952 officers' revolution which overthrew King Faruk and brought Gammel Abdel Nasser to power, the street was renamed Rue Bagdad. Streets often change names in the Levant, depending on how the political winds blow.

The apartment was well situated. There was a stop for Cairo's above ground metro only a few metres from the house. There was a florist on the ground floor. The Kashmir Cinema, which showed movies in Arabic, was walking distance, and the open-air Normandy Cinema, which had American and Italian films graced with both Arabic and French subtitles, was only one stop away. The fruit store and butcher were around the corner, and what food you could not get sometimes came to you on the street. This was primarily *ful medames*, the fava beans which were the staple of Egyptian cuisine and culture, which would arrive, by horse-pulled cart, in a huge copper pot every morning at 7.

But the crown jewel of the neighborhood was across the street. It was a French bakery, a patisserie, owned by a Greek family. It was called, if you can believe, Home Made Cake.

Now Cairo in those days was not only an ancient city with a storied past but was also the epitome of what we now refer to as a melting pot. Arabs, Greeks, French, Armenians, Brits, Copts, Turks, and Jews represented but a handful of the nations which filled the city streets. That melting pot was accompanied by all the respective languages - including English. But when my family spoke about Home Made Cake, I could not fathom a place with such a generic English name. Instead, I heard it in Arabic -

Om Met Kek.

As in "Ya wallad, je n'ais jamais manger un croque en bouche aussi bon que a Om Met Kek." My boy, I have never eaten as good a *croque en bouche* as I did at Om Met Kek.

My Tante Nandi, who lived down the road on Boutros Basha Gali, became misty eyed when talking about it. This from a woman who was famous for her own desserts. Her baklava and konafa were a thing of legend in our family.

"Ronnie," she would say, "your mother lived across from heaven. You can't believe how good the pastries were at Om Met Kek."

Om Met Kek.

Pronounced very quickly. With no pause between each word. As if it were only one word. It sounded like all the other Arabic names and expressions. I mean, in what world would there be a French patisserie in Cairo called Home Made Cake? I don't speak Arabic. I have learned a few words and phrases. I was pretty sure that Om meant mother. I just thought it was someone's name. Like the Swiss baker Groppi whose famed cafe with the eponymous name was the place to be seen for the pashas, beys, and doyens of Cairene society.

My father lived in north Heliopolis. My uncle Henri, my mother's brother, was his best friend. Every Sunday morning he would come for breakfast, and every Sunday he would stop at Home Made Cake before going back home in order to pick up pastries for his own family.

My mother came from a family of seven brothers and sisters. All but one, my Tante Gracia, who moved to Brazil, eventually landed in Montreal, Canada after being effectively thrown out of Egypt after the 1956 Suez Crisis. Although neither of my grandmothers, both of whom made the Atlantic crossing with their children, ever learned a single word of English, my father, mother, and all my aunts and uncles spoke it very well. My Tante Lilliane even worked as a French/English translator. My Tante Odette, who says she was so bad at math that she didn't qualify for the more academically rigorous Lycée Français, went to an Anglo/Arabic school. Tante Nandi became a bank manager and had to be proficient in French and English. Both my father and uncle Henri went to university and learned in English and Arabic. Although accented, they spoke English very well, with a rich vocabulary and proper grammar. I might be belaboring the point but I just want to make it clear they all spoke English very well.

But every time they spoke about the patisserie on rue Ismaili Pasha I never, not once, heard the words Home Made Cake.

Only Om Met Kek.

Of all the food my family was nostalgic about after leaving Egypt, the one they missed the most was not Egyptian at all. It was from Home Made Cake. And while they insist that everything in the store, which even had a convenient take out window, was absolutely delicious, the piece de resistance was the éclair. The only debate was if they preferred the chocolate or the coffee flavored filling. My Uncle Henri claimed they were the best eclairs in the world. His proclamations, delivered as if sermons from the mount, would often be a source of amusement for my father. But in this case, my father was a disciple. They were the best eclairs he had ever had. No éclair, not even the Duke de Gasgogne French bakery, could match those from their beloved Heliopolis patisserie.

To hear them tell it, the marvel of the éclair was not only the pastry and the filling - it was the size. The éclairs, they said, were huge. I was pretty sure it was a fisherman's tale rolled up in dough - the eclairs became bigger as each year went by.

"We used to cut them in three," my mother told me more than once.

I remember bringing a box of éclairs to the Egyptian poker group at the Hemispheres in Hallandale, Florida. They were, to be fair, from Publix, but they looked good. They thanked me for my gift but not as effusively as I had hoped. Only Tico had the guts to speak his mind.

"Ronnie," he said, "you need to understand. We ate éclairs from Om Met Kek. These are like a kick in the balls."

Om Met Kek

I had gone 60 years thinking that was what it was called and would have happily, inchaalah, gone another 60. And I would have were it not for a conversation I had with Tonto.

Tonto, in this case not the Lone Ranger's side kick, but the nickname my niece Danna has anointed to my Tante Odette. A nickname which the entire family has adopted. I called her to see how she was doing.

As usual she answered "Zay el zift merci," which means I am shit, thanks.

Which, as I said, is her default answer but this time she could lay some legitimate claim. She was recovering from her second broken hip and was cooped up in her apartment because of the pandemic. Her only guest was her son, my cousin, Morris, who brought her food and took her on short outings. So desperate was he to find her entertainment that he had taken to reading her some of my stories. Morris said I had gotten some good laughs, but instead of a compliment I got a complaint. Why did I not write more stories about Heliopolis and their lives in Egypt? I promised I would in my next book. I would even write about the great chocolate éclairs at Om Met Kek.

And she said "What?"

And I said "Om Met Kek."

And she said "De quoi tu parles?" What are you talking about?

And I said "The bakery across the street."

And she said. As clear as day. She said "Home Made Cake."

I said "Home Made Cake?"

She said "Oui. Home Made Cake." Again. Clear as day.

I said "I thought it was an Arabic name. Om Met Kek."

And then she laughed. But good. She couldn't get a word out she was laughing so hard.

When she could get a word out it was only to say "*majnoun*," which is 'crazy' in Arabic.

Then she said "Yalla bye," and hung up.

Ten minutes later the phone rang.
It was my cousin Morris.
"Hey Ron what's up?"
And I said "Just go ahead and say it."

"Say what?" He replied innocently. "Just get it over with."

"Ok," he said, "now listen closely. I am going to say it slowly:
 Home

Made

Cake."

And I said "I would kill for a chocolate éclair." And he said "Yeah,
me too."

TEN HOUSES

When I get back home from my walk I find my mother in the kitchen making her famous stuffed peppers.

This would ordinarily have given me considerable pleasure.

Except my mother has been dead for five years.

It is a bit of an existential crisis and one which I should confront immediately, but I really do love those stuffed peppers.

And not only has she come back from the dead, but she has brought spices and condiments with her.

So I decide to wait it out.

The peppers are as good as I remember, even better, no rust on her cooking at all. She has made a simple salad of lettuce, tomatoes, and cucumbers, oil and vinegar dressing, and has toasted a couple pieces of pita. We eat in silence. She makes a passing remark about my hair being too long but we mostly just eat without talking. I have missed these Egyptian dishes and am enjoying the combination of flavours and nostalgia. I am clearing the plates and loading the dishwasher when she finally announces the real reason for her visit.

"We did not let you go out for Halloween during the FLQ." She says, referring to the terrorist organization which in the fall of 1970 had kidnapped a British diplomat and murdered a Quebec politician, causing the prime minister, Pierre Elliot Trudeau to invoke the War Measures act.

"You have to change it."

So now I get it. She has not come back to cook. She has come back to edit.

She is referring to a new story I am working on called 'Ten Houses'. The plot hinges on me being allowed to trick or treat, but mostly to collect money for UNICEF, at ten houses on our block on the afternoon of Halloween during the October Crisis in 1970. I find a valuable coin in my Unicef box and have to decide whether to return it to its rightful and unsuspecting owner. It is a morality play which Jules, my actual editor whose culinary skills I am not privy to but who has the editorial distinction of actually being, you know, alive, and I have worked back and forth on. I think it turned out quite well.

"It's just to help the plot, mom," I explain. "It narrows down my search to ten houses. I needed a reason why I was only able to go to a few houses."

She holds up her hand in some sort of Egyptian 'don't go there' gesture, momentarily lifting it from the cup of Turkish coffee she has made from a 'canaka', a coffee pot, which I do not own.

"*Jamais de la vie*," she exclaims. "That would never happen."

And then, putting an exclamation mark on it, she says in Arabic *"bokra fel mish mish."* Which literally means 'when apricot season comes' but figuratively means 'when pigs fly'.

I try to explain how the stories mix fact and fiction but she is not having any of it.

"Jamais de la vie!" She repeats.

She then asks if I have any chocolate ice cream. I shake my head no. She arrives with peppers, stuffing, and Turkish coffee but no ice cream?

Then my father, who has been dead for fifteen years, appears in the living room, wearing his customary socks and sandals, holding a bowl of ice cream for me and a small cone for my mother.

He looks well all things considered.

"Show me the story," he says. I hand him the sheets. My father, though not really a fan of fiction, revered books and writing. He would set emotions aside and examine it rationally and pragmatically. I watch him read my story. I had a funny bit in the second paragraph and although it does not elicit a big laugh I do get a smile. I like that.

Then he looks up and says "It is nice to read about my old friend Taki." I nod my head. Taki was a colleague of my father's from work. I brought him into the story as the coin collector who happened to be at the house when I got back. He is the character who tells me the coin is valuable. Taki did not really collect coins. I just made that part up. But my father lets it go. He finishes reading and looks up.

"It is a morality play," he says.

I say "Yes."

"The boy discovers a valuable coin in his Unicef box and now has to decide if he gives it back."

"Exactly," I reply.

"It is a good story," he says.

I say "Thanks."

Then he says "Icarus," wagging his finger, "you flew too close to the sun."

"But I..." I stammer.

"That scene makes no sense," he says. "Nobody is going to believe we let you go out during the October Crisis."

"It was just ten houses," I argue.

"No." He shakes his head. "Look." He holds up the story and reads from it. "My mother was in charge of our costumes. But really, she was in charge of us not having costumes because she insisted my sister and I wear our winter parkas over any costume we had."

"Does that sound like someone who would let you go out of the house while there were kidnappings and murders?"

I shake my head no.

"That one inconsistency harms the entire story."

He is right. My buddy Harold Rosen would never believe it. There was no way I would have been allowed out. The story did not hold water.

I say "It is the 50-year anniversary of the October Crisis. And this year parents also have to decide whether to allow their kids to go trick or treating. I thought it would make a good story."

"Yes" he says. "It would make a good story. But this is not that story."

I say "Ok. I will change it."

He says, "Good. And maybe get a haircut too."

And then he and my mother disappear.

I never finished the story. Jules and I went back and forth a few times but I could never quite figure it out. By then I had a Goldfarb and Lewberg story which had a few good laughs so I eventually forgot about it altogether. Halloween came. I'm not sure how many kids went out. I can tell you nobody came to my house. I had bought some chocolate bars just in case but knew I was just going to eat them myself. But I didn't want chocolate bars. What I really wanted was a bowl of my mother's Syrian soup. A nice bowl of *chamd* with a scoop of rice.

I power up my laptop and open up a word document.

"This is the story about the time my mother let me go out and play in the middle of winter with wet hair."

Then I set the table and wait.

SCHWARTZMAN'S

Goldfarb and I were starving. We were sitting at my pool, doing our best not to ruin our appetite with a bag of Lay's salt and vinegar chips. It was 3:00pm already and Lewberg had not gotten back from Schwartzman's. Schwartzman's was a deli up in Pompano which specialized in Montreal style smoked meat sandwiches made famous by the Montreal restaurant whose name they had pretty much ripped off. The NY style pastrami and corned beef which abounded in South Florida could not hold a candle to the smoked meat we had grown up on and the quality at Schwartzman's quite honestly was as close to Schwartz's as was its name.

Anyway, Lewberg had hit his shot on number 15 into the water and thus earned the duty of going on the pick-up.

"Fucking Lewberg went for a drink," muttered Goldfarb. "Keep those chips away from me."

Goldfarb was likely right. Schwartzman's was located in a strip plaza right next to a gentleman's club called The Pleasure Dome. Truth be told, Lewberg wasn't a big fan of those sorts of establishments but the bar stocked Kettle vodka so he put aside whatever philosophical objections he had in favor of a strong drink.

I was about to curse him too but then he walked into the house. I didn't hear him or see him but I could smell the delicious combination of smoked meat, coleslaw, and potato salad.

"About fucking time," said Goldfarb.

"I got some extra karnatzle," said Lewberg. "Plus I emptied their fridge out of cream soda."

"Oh baby!" Exclaimed Goldfarb who had already forgiven Lewberg for his tardiness.

Then Lewberg said "Harold, have you been here all this time?"

And Goldfarb said "Where would I go?"

"Just checking. So I went into the bar to grab a quick Kettle and cran..."

Goldfarb turned to me and said "What did I tell you."

"...and I see this beige Crown Victoria in the VIP parking of the Dome. Right in front of the door."

"Crown Vic eh?" I said. "Nice. Old school. Just like Harold's."

Goldfarb said "The plaza has tons of parking. The guy can't walk twenty feet? Jesus people are so lazy!"

Lewberg said "Nope. VIP, right in front. But here's the thing - the Crown Vic had a personalized license plate."

"What did it say?" I asked.

"Well," replied Lewberg, "see for yourself." He pulled out his phone and laid it out on the table. Then he used two fingers to stretch and expand the photo so we could see it more clearly.

Florida plates.
With a name on them.
And the name was:z

Goldfarb

Goldfarb took a big bite of his sandwich and then grabbed a napkin in order to wipe off the excess mustard dribbling down his chin.

He said "Can I see that again?"

Lewberg slid him the phone.

Goldfarb said "Looks exactly like my car."

Lewberg said "I know. Even has your name."

"This is not good," said Goldfarb, shaking his head. "It is December 10th."

I said "What does the date have to do with anything?"

Goldfarb said "My cousin's daughter, Debbie, is getting married on the 20th. Every relative I have, aunts, uncles, nephews, nieces, are coming down to Florida from Canada."

"Is the reception at the Dome?" joshed Lewberg with a smile. "They actually have a great lunchtime buffet."

"Harold," I said, "You are overthinking it."

"I'm not overthinking it. I am thinking it. My entire family goes to Schwartzman's. They are going to see my car with my name in the parking lot of The Pleasure Dome."

"This is South Florida," I argued. "They are going to be eating near the beach."

Goldfarb said "Have you ever been to Torremolinos?"

"Michener put it on the map in The Drifters," offered Lewberg, who always surprised us with his breadth of knowledge. "Tourist town on the Spanish Riviera."

"Yes," agreed Goldfarb. "Huge tourist destination for the English vacationers. And do you know what these English vacationers like to eat when they are in Spain?"

I knew the answer. Even if I didn't know the answer, I knew there was only one place Goldfarb would be going with this.

"Fish and chips. They come all the way from Bristol, from Liverpool, from Manchester, in order to eat in English style pubs and restaurants serving the exact food they had just come from."

"Pompano isn't Torremolinos," I argued. Although I knew it was.

"My family will be going to Schwartzman's at least twice a week."

"Aren't there other Goldfarbs in your family?" Asked Lewberg.

"Nope. Just me. My dad was an only child. All my relatives are from my mother's side. I'm the only Goldfarb. In fact, I'm the only Goldfarb I know."

"Except for the guy in the VIP parking at the Pleasure Dome," I said.

"Maybe he won't be there again," said Lewberg hopefully.

"Yeah, maybe," I said.

But we both knew that was wishful thinking.

The next day, we squeezed into Lewberg's convertible at around 12:30 and headed to Pompano. The three of us had all put on long pants for the occasion. Goldfarb had exchanged his usual slides for a pair of sneakers and one of us, I won't say who, might have even been wearing cologne. We parked across from Schwartzman's and walked to the Pleasure Dome. It was, as Goldfarb had argued, only a few metres away. As we had feared, the beige Crown Victoria was parked in the VIP spot. The doorman, who was marking up a program for the nearby Pompano dog track, asked, without looking up, for $2 for parking. Goldfarb, showing remarkable restraint, pulled out two dollar bills and handed them to the doorman without making an argument about having to pay for free parking.

"Can you tell me who owns that beige Crown Victoria over there?" I asked, pointing to it.

The doorman said "I don't think I remember."

Then Lewberg, in a move so deft it was hard not to assume he had performed it dozens of times before, snatched the bills right out of the doorman's hand and replaced them with a twenty.

"I can't even remember what I had for lunch yesterday," he said with a smile.

"I like this dog in the seventh," said the doorman. "Same name as my first wife, Mildred. She could run like the wind." He circled the name on the program then looked up and said "New owner. Bought the place last month. For another $20 I can tell you his name."

The doorman had a pretty good sense of humor.

The Dome was very dark, very smoky, and was playing very loud music I suspected was also used on Guantanamo Bay prisoners. It had a long bar and a buffet set up in the back. There was nobody on the stage and, save for two women I presumed to be dancers sitting at the bar who were busy on their phones and sharing what looked to be a plate of nachos, we were the only people in the entire place. The dancers looked up, I want to say briefly, but it was even shorter than that, when we walked in but then went back to their phones and nachos. In other words, pretty much like any other bar we had ever been in.

The waitress, who already looked like she was counting the hours remaining in her shift, came and took our orders. Goldfarb had his diet coke. Lewberg his Kettle and cran. And I, knowing better than to order a Guinness in a place like this, ordered a Bud Light I knew I would not drink.

When she came back with our orders, Goldfarb asked if we could see the manager.

She said "Hey, I don't make the prices. But I don't blame you, $15 for a freakin' Bud."

Goldfarb said "No, no, the prices are fine. We just wanted to ask him about his car."

"Oh, ok hon."

Two minutes later a man came out. I'm not sure what we were expecting but he was tall and lanky with a full moustache. He was wearing a vest with a huge Lonestar state belt buckle. He looked a little, actually a lot, like the actor Sam Elliot who, amongst other things, played a cowboy in *The Big Lebowski*. Later, in the car ride back, we would all agree he looked like a cowboy. What he did not look like was a Goldfarb.

But, that is who he was. Oscar Goldfarb. Those were the first words out of his mouth when he came to our table and shook our hands.

The second words were "I'll take $50,000 for the car and I'll throw in my Waylon Jennings Greatest Hits CD". Then he winked and said "Truth is, that sonabitch has been stuck in there for two weeks."

Goldfarb said "I'm not so much interested in the car as I am the license plate." He took out his wallet from his pocket and removed his driver's license. "You see," he handed Oscar Goldfarb his license, "my name is Harold Goldfarb."

And Oscar Goldfarb said "No shit. Look at that we are mishpocha," which was maybe the way Jews from Texas pronounced it.

"Yes," answered Goldfarb, "and as mishpocha," Goldfarb delicately pronouncing it, "I wonder if you could do me a favor."

"Anything for a landsman," said Oscar Goldfarb.

"Well," continued Goldfarb, "my family from Canada is coming to Florida next week."

"Canada," exclaimed Oscar Goldfarb. "I heard it was colder than a witch's tit. You couldn't get a pack of wild horses to drag me there."

"Well yes," said Goldfarb tiptoeing through the cliché landmines. "There is a family wedding."

"Mazal tov," said Oscar Goldfarb.

"Thank you," said Goldfarb. "And the family all love to go to Schwartzman's."

"The brisket is to die for," said Oscar Goldfarb.

"It is," said Goldfarb. "The thing is, I also have a beige Crown Victoria and my name is also Goldfarb, and so with your car and its plates parked out front they might get the...."

Oscar Goldfarb held up his hand. "Say no more. You don't need your family thinking that you are spending the day getting, how should I say, getting the wrong type of *naches*. I will park in the back. I could use the walk."

"Thank you, Oscar," said Goldfarb. "I really appreciate it."

"Are you kidding. We Goldfarbs gotta stick together. Let me get you another round of drinks. Maybe you want to meet a couple of the ladies."

"Thanks Oscar," said Goldfarb. "We'll have to take a rain check. Another time. We have a tee time this afternoon."

"Well I envy you. I schlepped my sticks all the way down from Jacksonville and haven't had a chance to play yet. You guys hit them straight. Hell, I'm going to move the car now. Better safe than sorry."

Since we were already here, we decided to have lunch at Schwartzman's. Goldfarb and I had tuna, but Lewberg, who embodied the 'when in Rome' life philosophy, loaded up on smoked meat.

"Well, that was easy," I said.

"Yeah, nice guy," said Lewberg.

"Maybe too easy?" Questioned Goldfarb.

"Sometimes things work out Harold," I said.

"Yeah, maybe you're right," he said, helping himself to half of Lewberg's sandwich. "Hey, you think he was angling for a golf invite?"

"I think he was just being polite," I said.

"Would be a fun guy to play with," Lewberg said, "and the place was empty. He might have a window for 9 holes."

Goldfarb said "Yeah. Wouldn't hurt to ask." He got up and I held up my hand and said "You know what Harold, I'll go, you stay here and pay the bill."

And Goldfarb said "Fair enough. It is the least that I can do."

So I went back to the Dome, paid the doorman another $2 for not parking, allowed my eyes to adjust to the light, and found Oscar Goldfarb behind the main bar. The two dancers were still on their phones. This time they did not even look up.

"Hey partner," he said, "you forget something?"

"We just thought we would invite you to join us for golf this afternoon."

"Well that's mighty kind of you. But I have a contractor coming in this afternoon so I have to stay at my post. Doing some big renovations for the grand re-opening. My turn to take a rain check."

I said "Ok. Anytime."

Lewberg and I didn't really know Goldfarb's cousin Debbie but Goldfarb didn't want to go alone so he scored us an invite to the wedding anyway. It was at the Four Seasons on the beach in Fort Lauderdale and Harold had promised us killer apps and an open bar. Lewberg, in a moment of graciousness, said yes without even asking if they were going to stock Kettle. Goldfarb, looking better than he had in years, was in a tux. In addition to looking good, he was feeling good.

"Five days in a row," he said. "At least one member of my family ate at or picked up food from Schwartzman's five days in a row."

"No sign of the Crown Vic?" I asked.

"Nada. Parked all the way in the back. I checked it out myself."

"Oscar did you a solid," I said.

"Damn straight," replied Goldfarb as he adjusted his tie. "Jesus, I look great! For once a family function which doesn't blow up in my face."

Lewberg and I, though the invitation said black tie, were in sports jackets. Truthfully, we were looking pretty good too. Goldfarb was not lying about the pre-ceremony appetizers. We all basically made a meal of the lollipop lamb chops after positioning ourselves in the exact spot where the wait staff came out of the kitchen. They had set up chairs and the *chuppah* right on the edge of the beach and it really was beautiful. We told Goldfarb we would watch the ceremony from the back row but we slipped out and had a drink at the hotel bar instead. The drinks weren't free but we were spared 45 minutes of aisle marching, endless vows, and readings in Aramaic, Hebrew, and English.

We snuck back in just as the groom stepped on the glass and was greeted with a chorus of *l'chayims*.

It was also at the exact same time the small prop plane, dragging an advertising banner, like the type which routinely dotted the skies above the beach, appeared above our heads.

Everyone looked up at the same time. I had to admit, it was a catchy banner.

"Goldfarb's Strip Club: Let our talented dancers show you what mazel really is."

THE RUMOUR

Photograph © Darren Tunnicliff

I have since cut down a lot but there was a time when I used to have quite a lot of sugar with my coffee. This prompted friends, family, and the occasional waiter to make a joke which I heard so often that I would often be surprised if it was not made at all.

"Why don't you have some coffee with your sugar." Which is funny enough and I laughed the first hundred times I heard it.

This story is from back before I cut down. I think it might have been in 1990. I was having a cafe latte, the Israelis call it a cafe affouch, an upside-down coffee, in one of those outside patios which line Dizingoff. At the table next to me was an older man, with a trimmed grey beard and beat-up black beret which was more working-class than bohemian. He wore a suit as these old-timers tended to but had, in a tip of the beret to the country where he was now living, removed his tie. He had availed himself of the free newspapers which the cafe provided to its patrons-he had the Jerusalem Post, Haaretz, both in English, plus one in what I presumed to be Russian and another in Hebrew. It looked like he was going to make an afternoon of it. I did not begrudge him. I too had nursed many a coffee or beer for the better part of an afternoon in order to lengthen an enjoyable stay.

The cafe had those cylindrical sugar packets you often see in Europe and I had already poured a couple into my coffee and had ripped the opening of a third. I had seen him eying me and had the feeling he had been biting his tongue. That he had something he wanted to say.

My Hebrew was not that good but I had kind of figured out what the equivalent of 'why don't you have some sugar with your coffee' was in Hebrew and so that was what I was expecting him to say when he finally addressed me.

But when he did address me, it was not in Hebrew but in a Russian accented English.

And what he said was "You should be shot for using so much sugar."

Which was funny. And would have been funny. Had he not been so serious. But I laughed anyway.

"If you don't mind me asking." He said, "what is it you do which allows you to be so generous with your sugar?"

We both knew the sugar packets were free. But we also both knew what he meant.

"I'm a writer," I said. I wasn't. But I could have been.

"A writer," he said "hoo whah. Well, Mr writer. If you have a few shekels to buy me a chocolate babka, I will tell you a story about sugar."

I had a few shekels.

This is the story he told me.

The rumour started at the chess club on Suvevorov Street. Not in the club, but on the roof of the four-story building that housed the club. A mid-March day had burst into double digits, Boris insisted it was 12 degrees, and tables, chairs and boards had been moved onto the roof in order to soak in the rare Moscow sun. Some of the men had taken off their shirts. All were men who should not be taking off their shirts even when showering or in the sauna. But it was 12 degrees and the sun was shining, Sicilian Defences were being played, Queens were being sacrificed and shirts were being discarded. Eventually, it was just Larianov and a man we knew only as The Bull for reasons which were not clear. Nothing in his physique, for he too had bared his torso, where dangled a gold star of David, would lead anyone to think it was an apt nickname. So we watched and kibitzed and insulted each others' play and flabby bodies until someone, it was probably Boris, it was nearly always Boris, said he heard there might be some sugar.

Both Larianov and The Bull stopped playing, even slapping down a meaty hand on the timer so no one would be penalized, and looked up at Boris demanding to know what he knew and where he had heard from.

Like a fine piece of art, every rumour had its own provenance, often long and circuitous and complicated but, unlike a painting, which only needed one shady ownership to put the entire provenance in question, a rumour only needed one credible monger in its coterie to make it viable. In this case, it was Micha. Boris said he had heard it from Micha. Micha had a cousin who had a friend whose mother-in-law worked as a cleaning lady at a dacha, a summer house, on the Caspian Sea belonging to a Party member. It was not, all things considered, for a Russian rumour, that many degrees of separation, which gave us some optimism but mostly we were buoyed because it had come from Micha.

Now Micha's average on rumours was still well below the Mendoza line - less than 1 in 5- but the key was he had been right about his last rumour, the raincoats. Now none of us had gotten a raincoat, though we had all stood in line, some of us for eight hours, mostly in an ironic pouring rain, but there was no question that there were raincoats to be had- we had seen people coming out of the store happily waving a washed-out red raincoat which from even where we were standing, back near the end of the line, we could see were clearly too small for the lucky recipient and would only fit a child, but they were raincoats nonetheless. But Micha had been right the last time and, in the rumour game, in the Russian rumour game, you were only as good as your last rumour, so now his sugar rumour, by way of Boris, carried a little bit more weight.

"I bet it is Bulgarian sugar," spat out Anton Mickeilovitch "I wouldn't feed Bulgarian sugar to my dog."

We all knew Anton Mickeilovitch did not own a dog and that he would likely give his left arm for a kilo of Bulgarian sugar but nobody pushed back because Anton Mickeilovitch had lost his wife and his brother in the last year and we all knew that even a kilo of sugar, Bulgarian or otherwise, could not sweeten his bitterness.

"Maybe it will be Latvian sugar," mused Larianov as he moved his knight to b7. This drew a hearty laugh from the crowd. Latvian sugar had near mythical aura about it. It was said that Khrushchev had built a factory just outside of Riga which produced such fine grains of sugar that they were like a Tahitian beach. Not a rat dropping ever made its way into the giant vats. His cook made him khvorost, angel wings of fried dough with powdered sugar, every night for dessert. None of us had ever seen it. None of us had tasted it. Had never known anyone who had seen it or tasted it. Even if it did exist, there was no way it would land into the hands of us patzers. Still, it was nice to dream.

No, if the rumour was true, and we were a long way from that, it would be Russian sugar. More brown than white. More pebble than grain. The factory was close to the Aral Sea which caused many people to say more salty than sweet.

In Moscow, nine out of the ten times we stood in a line, we did not know what we were standing in line for. Moscow was a city of people lining up for things. It did not matter what it was because it was surely something you needed. Because we needed everything. Or, at the very least, something you could trade for something you needed. Most of the time, you would get to the front of the line and they would have run out of the thing even before you knew what the thing was. Most of the time, you wouldn't get to the front of the line.

Boris's Misha rumour was of no use without knowing where this sugar would be distributed. Which store. Which stores. The sugar would surely not fall from the sky.

The sugar was the rumour.

The store. Well, the store was the information.

All the chess players on the roof understood that the rumour was as free as the air they breathed. They also understood that the information was no longer useful information if everyone knew about it. This was how it worked. They were not bitter. Even Anton Mickeilovitch, who could give the marror we ate on Passover a run for its money, was not bitter about it. Not more bitter than he already was. We knew there was a long line to wait in even before we could get to the line we would stand-in. If there was sugar and if there was really a location where it was being sold, the cleaning lady would know first and she would tell the people she would tell. They would then, in turn, tell the people they would tell. She would likely tell her son-in-law who would also tell the people he would tell and they the people they would tell. Maybe the son in law would tell his friend, Misha's cousin, and maybe then maybe Misha's cousin would tell Misha who in turn tell Boris. By then, a lot of people would be standing in line for what they hoped to be low-grade sugar the majority of the world would not feed to their dogs. While in line, but not a minute before, they would tell friends and family in the hope that when there would be another line they could say "hey remember when I told you about the sugar."

By the time Boris found out from Misha where the sugar was being distributed, there had been many more rumours. Everyone had a mother-in-law. Everyone had a cousin. Most of us had friends. Boris was my friend so I found out before he got in line but a long time after most of the rest of Moscow also got in line.

We knew after an hour there was no sugar. Not Latvian. Not Bulgarian. Not Russian. But an hour was not a long time and although we were not near the front, we were certainly not all the way in the back. And the sun was shining, a couple of us had brought our chess boards, and a couple of others had brought some vodka. This is only to say that when The Bull walked up and said he had heard a rumour about a line for tractor parts, nobody paid him much attention. We all lived in the city. None of us owned a tractor. And although we could maybe trade a tractor part for something else, we had pretty much decided to settle on the two sugars in the bush. So we all said no and returned to our games but then The Bull nudged me with his knee and said I should come with him to get a tractor part. And I said, I don't want a tractor part. And anyway, it is not a tractor part but a line for a tractor part. Then The Bull held up his own portable chess board and pieces and said "I will spot you a pawn and a bishop.

And I thought that was a strange thing to say because The Bull really hated to lose and although he was a much, much better player than me I was good enough to beat him if he spotted me a pawn and a bishop. So I went with him.

With that, the old Russian man drained his coffee and delicately wiped the chocolate babka crumbs from his beard and moustache. He had told this story before. This is where he paused for dramatic effect. I was ok with that. I didn't mind being a pawn in his game.

"Did you get a tractor part?" I asked.

He shook his head no.

"Sugar?" I liked this ending. That would have been my ending. Sugar at the tractor parts store. So classic.

But he shook his head no.

"So nu?" I asked, invoking the ancient Yiddish admonition.

He smiled and said "Exit visa."

Exit visa.

"That's how you got out of the country?"

"Yes."

"And the tractor parts store?"

"Was the Brazilian consulate. The Bull, whose name was Meyer Meyerovitch, had heard a rumour of 20 exit visas. He was number 19 and I was 20."

"Good story," I said.

"You will write it?" He asked.

"Yes," I answered. "I will write it."

And now, nearly 30 years later, I have.

THE PITCH

It was the end of a long day and I was looking forward to hitting a few balls and then taking a *shvitz*. I was packing up and getting ready to go when my partner, Barry Leviticus, walked into my office. He did not look happy. Barry had been my partner for nearly twenty years.

Together, the two of us had built the biggest pr/marketing agency in all of Babylonia - Leviticus and Numbers. We were descendants from the people who had been exiled. While most of us went back, our families stayed behind and made a life together here.

It was a great partnership. I was the ideas guy and Barry took care of finance. It is a bit ironic because my name is Numbers, Mendel Numbers. It was Barry though who was the happiest taking care of the financials. Sometimes that's just the way it goes in the public relations game. But now, Barry did not look happy. I had seen that look before when we couldn't make payroll but that couldn't be the case because we were flush with cash.

Anyway, I was about to find out because you could say what you wanted about Barry Leviticus but he didn't beat around the burning bush.

"They want us to pitch," he said.

Getting asked to pitch was usually a good thing. It was only bad if it was an existing client.

"Who wants us to pitch?" I asked but I was afraid I already knew.

"The Board. They are coming in at 9 am. They want a brand-new campaign. Something fresh. Something which will excite the younger demographic."

The Board was our biggest account. For five years we had handled all of their branding and publicity. They used to have an in-house guy but 5 years ago I convinced them to take us on. They now represented 50% of our total business. This was my fault. Instead of going out and getting new business I had coasted and rested on my laurels.

"Ok," I said. "This isn't a disaster. We can do this."

"Mendel," said Barry, "they are taking other meetings. Word is they are meeting with other agencies."

"Jumping Jehoshavus!" I said. "Please tell me they aren't meeting with Bartholomew and Mathew." B and M were our biggest rivals. They had created the greatest marketing campaign of all time. Just this morning I had drunk coffee from a 'walk on water' mug.

"I don't know. But it doesn't look good."

"Don't panic Barry," I said. "I'll come up with something."

So much for golf and a steam. I would have to pull an all-nighter. Well, it wouldn't be the first time. I went to make myself a cup of coffee but remembered the canister was empty. This morning I had reused the grounds I had fished out from the garbage along with the old filter. I would have to do that again. It had been gross but drinkable; coffee was Barry's responsibility. Barry had better buy new coffee in time for the Board.

The Board showed up at 9 on the nose. Four of them. In formal suits. Barry and I stood nervously as they made their way into our conference room.

"I can't tell one Cohen from another," I whispered.

"Will you shut up!" Barry hissed back.

I took drink orders. Two black coffees, one with cream, and one tea with honey. Barry had picked up crullers along with coffee on the way to the office. I served the hot drinks in our own promotional mugs. They were adorned with the slogan which we, actually, which I had come up with, five years ago in our first pitch meeting.

They tried to kill us. We won. Let's eat.

I was proud of it. It had won awards. It was a classic. Who would want to mess around with a classic.

We started with small talk.

"Mendel, how is your game?" Asked one of the board members.

"Can't get rid of that slice. You will have to let me take you out to the club."

"I would love to. But it is our busy season. A lot of anointing. I am booked back to back"

Barry could not brook much small talk.

41

"Are we losing your account?" He blurted out.

"Chas v'shalom. Heaven forbid!" Said one of the board members. "We love Leviticus and Numbers. We are just looking for a little rebranding for one of our products."

Well this wasn't the disaster I expected. Barry had worried me for nothing.

"Which product?" I asked.

"Hanukkah," said one of the board members.

Hanukkah. I wasn't surprised. Their in-house guy had completely butchered the message. Here we were in the fifth century and there was still a debate about the spelling. It was a nightmare. We had gone a long way in repairing the brand. Last year we launched Maccabi action figures. But these things take time. It was not an easy sell. For now, we had lumped Hanukkah together with Purim as part of our 'they tried to kill us we won let's eat' campaign. But Purim was an easier sell. It was a no brainer - a clear-cut hero. A clear-cut villain. Costume parties and drinking. That product sold itself. Hanukkah was much tougher. It had been a great victory but had come with costs.

"Ok," I said, "we can come up with something. How much time do we have?"

One of the Board said "No time. This is the pitch."

Leviticus asked if anyone wanted another cruller. Everyone had a second helping. They were delicious.

"What's your goal here?" I asked.

"We would like to have greater participation. Especially amongst the younger demographic. You have seen the numbers. We just can't get any traction."

I had seen the numbers. They weren't good.

"Drinking is always good," suggested Leviticus.

"No more drinking," declared one of the Cohens. Between Purim and the four cups at Pesach our people are becoming shickers."

I thought about it.

"How about gambling?"

The Cohens spoke amongst themselves.

"Gambling we can live with," they declared.

"Maybe a little gift giving?" I suggested. "Presents are very popular these days."

"We don't want to commercialize it," said one of the Board.

"Well, we could cap it at 20 shekels. Just a token."

"I think we can live with that," he said.

I stood up and walked to the big calendar on our white board. A lot of the holidays were bunched together in the same months in the fall.

"How married are you to the date?" I asked.

The Cohens again talked amongst themselves.

"We are flexible about the date," one finally said. "What do you have in mind?" I pointed to the empty white space in December. "Let's move it to December. It will have the entire month to itself. Nothing to compete with. No other distractions."

"Except for the birthday," mumbled Leviticus.

That was true. There was the birthday. B and M had done such a good job on that campaign. The way they stretched it out.

The Cohens mumbled amongst themselves. The birthday was a bit of a sore spot.

Although...

"Although," I said, "maybe we can leverage with something for ourselves."

"There can be no birthday," declared one of the board members.

"No," I said. I was now on a roll. This is why they paid me the big bucks. "Not a birthday. A miracle. What we need here is a miracle."

The Cohens all nodded their heads. They were big fans of miracles.

"But what could it be?"

And then I remembered the coffee I had made with the discarded filter.

"How bout this. The Maccabees recaptured the temple and wanted to light the ceremonial candles but there was only enough oil for one night. The miracle is that the oil lasted for three nights."

"Three nights isn't much of a miracle," said Leviticus. "What about eight?"

"I love it," I said, "and we light one extra candle every night." Now I was cooking with gas.

"We can make promotional items. Coffee mugs, key chains, mouse pads. With a new slogan." I held up my hand as if in thought. But I had already come up with it.

"A Big Miracle Happened Here"

The Cohens repeated it to themselves. A big miracle happened here. It was gold. Sometimes, in the middle of a pitch, you just know that you nailed it. We got the thumbs up. They were clearly thrilled with our idea.

They got up to leave. We all shook hands.

"When can you show us a deck?" One asked.

"Let me bring in design and analytics. I should have something for you in two days."

We said our goodbyes. There was excitement in the air.

As he was walking out the door one of the Cohens turned back and said, "Those crullers were delicious. Maybe see if you can include something with fried dough."

And I said "I'll see what I can do."

SILVER TWEEZERS

Photograph © Sergey Ryzhov / 123rf.com

I have started, more by accident than anything, collecting stamps. I had been thinking about writing a short story about a character who tries to impress a woman by getting his face on a stamp. It turned out though that you could order customized stamps with your face on them from the post office so it sort of made the idea a little less compelling. But by the time I found out, I had already bought a few books about stamp collecting and even ordered a few packs of stamps from Amazon in order to get started. I was now going to collect stamps. I went to my friend David's house and he showed me some of his Israeli stamps. I recognized many as stamps my father had collected and it brought back some warm memories. David asked me what I was planning to collect. Was there some sort of theme or category? I said I really didn't know. Maybe stamps from places I had lived in or visited he suggested. And I said yeah, that might be a good idea. We had lived in Singapore for 2 years and I was interested in the history of the region. So I went back home and started looking up stamps from Singapore and from Malaysia. I wasn't looking for anything specific but then I stumbled upon the twenty-five-cent Malaysia. I knew that stamp.

This is a picture of the twenty-five-cent stamp from Malaysia. If you look closely, you can see the year. 1972. That is when I first saw it. I was thirteen. It was three weeks after my bar mitzvah. I was seeing it again 48 years later.

My father like, I suspect, many men of his generation, collected stamps. He did not buy stamps. He did not trade stamps. He did not go to stamp shows or correspond with other stamp collectors. He only collected stamps from envelopes he himself received in the mail. He was very fastidious about that. This, he believed, was how stamps should be collected. Our family and the few friends he had knew this, and would always send a letter, never a postcard, whenever they traveled abroad. He had a nice collection, and while most of the stamps were from Israel and Canada, he had stamps from an impressive list of countries. All teased from letters he had personally received in the mail.

He soaked the envelopes in a bowl of water, gently and delicately removed them with silver tweezers which had once belonged to his father, dried them on a red checkered terry cloth towel, then finally pressed them between volumes of the 1970 World Book

Encyclopedia. I think it was letters N and M, as they were the heftiest. He then put them in a stamp album. The albums, they were olive green, were arranged chronologically. He had no categories. Did not separate by country. He entered the stamps as he received them. He would work on his stamps on Sunday mornings after a breakfast of ful (fava beans which are an Egyptian staple) and pita, hard boiled-eggs, and raw onions.

He collected stamps. That is just what he did. I never heard him talk about it. He never pulled out his albums to share with guests. I would sit with him on the kitchen table after my mother had cleared the remains of Egyptian days gone by. I did not eat *ful* in those days but Sunday was sweet cereal day - usually Cap'n Crunch, so I looked forward to it as much as my father did.

I don't remember having conversations with my father during those mornings. If we did, it would have been hard to hear because the Grundman record player would be blasting, well, blasting might be an exaggeration - Beethoven or Mozart, or Schubert. He knew all the music intimately and would sometimes close his eyes in bliss in anticipation of a passage. He would praise the piece, speaking words in French or sometimes, if the music really moved him, in Italian, and I would nod my head in agreement. No other words were exchanged. We just went along with our business and I would be given unspoken tasks.

He let me rip the corners off the envelopes, let me soak those corners in the bowl of water. He let me fold over the terrycloth towel and pat the stamps in an effort to speed up the drying process. He let me put the stamps in between the volumes of the encyclopedia, and I would look up at his face to see if today he would be ok with me sitting on the encyclopedia - depending on his mood - in order to really flatten the stamps. In time, he even let me enter the stamps into the album.

But he never let me touch the tweezers.

I don't think it was because he didn't trust me. I think it was because it was the task which gave him the most pleasure. He attacked it with surgical precision, angling a bedside lamp he carried into the kitchen just to have the best lighting. Truth is, most of the stamps quickly detached themselves from the envelope and ended up floating like lily pads in the bowl where they could easily be scooped up and laid out on the towel. But sometimes the stamp glue proved too stubborn and my father would pull out the tweezers. We both knew that another twenty minutes of soaking would probably do the trick but we also both knew it would deprive my father of the pleasure.

He would hold up the impeccably extracted stamp, hinges perfectly intact, and say "ah ha" as I stared wide-eyed. My bar mitzvah was coming up in a few weeks and, along with being called up to the Torah, I hoped a turn with the tweezers would be my rite of passage. The family was all abuzz about my bar mitzvah. For all the usual reasons but also because my father had invited Terry Humphreys.

Terry Humphreys was my father's boss. Somehow the subject of my bar mitzvah had come up in the lunchroom. Terry Humphreys said he had never been to a bar mitzvah. He was, he said, very interested in Jewish rituals. My father nodded his head and that is where it would have ended if my Uncle Henri, who had been quietly eating my Tante Nandi's *poulet soffrito* and *fasulia* out of a large red Tupperware, had not decided to pipe up and say, "You should come to the bar mitzvah." Which really left my father no choice.

I'm not sure what the French or Arabic equivalent of 'throwing someone under the bus' is, but it would have been pointless to say it in either because my Uncle Henri was convinced he had just done my father a huge favor. Either way, I had gone from the most nervous person in the Zevy family - I was reciting all the prayers, my *haftorah*, reading from the Torah, and had a speech to give to boot - to being a distant runner up.

At issue was who to sit Terry Humphreys and his wife, Clara, with. He would obviously be with my Uncle Henri and his wife, my Tante Nandi, but then who? Terry Humphreys and his wife Clara would be, aside from my friend Stevie Sheen, the only non-Jews. For a while, my father thought of inviting more colleagues from work and creating a Sherwin Williams table. But my mother convinced him the late invite would be in bad taste. In the end, he chose my Uncle Roger and Aunt Mira. Both were Egyptian Jews but Uncle Roger had grown up in England and had just a hint of an English accent. It was the best we could come up with.

In the end, it did not matter because Terry Humphreys had to cancel because he was going on a business trip to Malaysia. So, I went back to being the most nervous family member, had a bar mitzvah which went off more or less without a hitch, and did not think of Terry Humphreys until three weeks after my bar mitzvah when a very fat envelope, postmarked Malaysia, arrived in the mail. I tore into it and discovered a very nice note and 100 US dollars. It turns out that when Terry Humphreys asked my Uncle Henri what the appropriate bar mitzvah gift was Uncle Henri had replied "Cash is traditional." Which is not entirely true but he was doing me a solid. $100 was a shit-load of money in those days. Until then, the best gift I had received was a Sanyo cassette player from my Tante Racheline and Uncle Solly.

After much debate and discussion, my father agreed I would put 50 in the bank and could spend the other 50 - I had my eye on a mini pool table - on whatever I wanted. My father then handed me the envelope which had contained the magical hundred dollars and said "We don't have stamps from Malaysia." Little did we know that three years later we would be living on the Malaysian peninsula in the city-state of Singapore.

I only soaked the envelope for ten minutes. I knew what I was doing. I wanted to use those tweezers. But the stamp, the Malaysia twenty-five cent, was not ready to come off. I ripped it in two.

I had gone from elation to fighting off tears. Stamps were holy in our house. My father handled them like newborn babies. We could no more rip a stamp than we could rip a page from the Torah I had read from three weeks earlier. My father walked over from the sink where he had been scrubbing a pot and examined the damage. I braced myself for a stern lecture but it never came. "Those other two stamps are nice," he said, referring to the other Malaysian stamps which had been on the envelope. "Soak them for ten more minutes and we'll try again." But the stamps detached themselves in the water all by themselves and I never got to use those silver tweezers. Not that day and never again. I still sat with my father some Sundays and performed my tasks. But then I stopped - interests took me elsewhere. I think he may have stopped at some point too. I was much, much older before I realized it probably didn't have anything to do with collecting stamps after all.

I order the twenty-five-cent Malaysia from HipStamp for $3.25. It arrives four weeks later from a dealer in New Jersey. It takes me fifteen minutes to extract it from the cocoon where it has been safely ensconced.

It's nice. I look at it through my newly acquired magnifying glass. Nice. It is mint. Then I put it in my blue stamp album.

The stamps on the envelope from New Jersey are US 32 cents. They are of a soccer ball and a basketball. I already have four copies of those but I diligently tear the corner along with those of the other envelopes I received this morning and drop them into the popcorn bowl I use as a soaker.

The doorbell rings and it is my friend Downtown Darren Brown. We chat on the front porch for a while and by the time I get back into the house the stamps are already detached and doing the backstroke on top of the bowl.

I use my new silver tweezers to pluck them out of the water. I put the stamps in my olive green album.

I SHALL BE RELEASED

The Angel of Death is at my door. I start to shake. To his credit, he mollifies my fears right away. "No, no. I just need to use your bathroom. I have been on the job all night and haven't had a chance. I'm just bursting dude." I tell him be my guest. He rushes by me and makes a beeline for the bathroom.

I hear the water run. I guess the Angel of Death washes his hands.

He comes out wiping his hands on his trousers.

"A roll of paper towel wouldn't kill you. No pun intended. It's just good hygiene."

I tell the Angel of Death "My bad. I don't get many guests."

He says "It's all good. I see you read the New York Times. Interesting." I had read the Sunday Book Review on the toilet. I left it in the bathroom.

I say "The book review. Hoping they review something I have written one of these days." I don't know why I am telling the Angel of Death my hopes and dreams. I guess I am a little nervous.

He says "They won't print my letters to the editor. That Friedman doesn't have a clue." I don't know if he is just fucking with me.

The Angel of Death looks at his watch. He has a gold Rolex. He says "Listen, I've got a thing I need to do in about an hour. Do you think I can hang here?"

I say "Um."

"It's just I need to be close by. For this thing I need to do."

"In the building?" I ask. "You have a thing to do in this building?"

"I can't say. Just for," he checks his watch again, "57 minutes."

"Right, right. Sorry. I was just wondering. Of course you can stay. Can I get you a drink?"

"Do you have something peaty?"

I give him an 18-year-old Laphroaig. As I hand him the glass he says "Corner three bedroom".

I say "Really?"

He puts his finger to his lips and says "You didn't hear it from me."

The Angel of Death eyes the ivory chess set I have on my coffee table - it is really more decorative than anything.

"Game?" He suggests.

I look up and say "We have less than hour." The Angel of Death smiles and says "It won't take that long. Fischer was one of mine. Let's just say we took the long way home. He taught me a few things on the way."

The Angel of Death plays pawn to king 4. I make my move in reply.

"Sicilian Defence. Nice. This might take me a few more minutes than I thought."

I say "My father loved the Sicilian."

"Ah Marco," he says and my heart skips a beat. But before I can ask him anything, he spots my record collection and walks over to the shelf.

The Angel of Death now starts rifling through my record albums. He admires my turntable. "Old school eh? I haven't seen one of these in ages."

Old school eh? Is the Angel of Death Canadian?

"Yeah," I say. "I guess I am a bit of an audiophile."

The Angel of Death pulls out The Band's Music from Big Pink. "Oh man," he says. "Are you fucking kidding me. I love this. Can we put this on?"

I say "Be my guest. You don't get to listen to music where," I struggle to find the right words "where you come from?"

The Angel of Death gently places the vinyl on the turntable and ever so delicately lowers the needle.

"The old man has a thing for musicals," he says, not hiding his contempt. "I mean, I love Hamilton as much as the next guy but could you give me a break for the love of... well you know."

I say "Yeah," but I don't really.

We sit and listen to The Band. I help myself to my own pour of Laphroaig and top up the Angel of Death's glass. It gives me a chance to get a better look at him. He has the requisite goatee and a cowlick which looks like it is held down by gel. He is wearing khakis and a button-down shirt. If I didn't know he was the Angel of Death I would have guessed he was an assistant manager at Whole Foods.

I haven't listened to The Band for a long time too and the combination of music and scotch is creating a nice vibe.

We sing the chorus of *The Weight* together.

"Take a load off Fanny

Take a load for free

Take a load off Fanny

And and, and... you put the load right on me"

The Angel of Death has a nice voice. It is the last song on the first side. We sit in silence for a minute and then the Angel of Death starts chuckling.

"The old man was convinced it was Annie," he says. "Take a load off Annie. We had a huge fight about it. He almost had me go get Robbie Robertson to settle it. I had to talk him out of it. Talk about stubborn."

"Jesus," I say.

"Yeah. He put me on earthquakes for a year after that. Backbreaking work. I can tell you. He said it had nothing to do with it but you do the math." Then he flips the album and we listen to the other side.

When *I Shall Be Released* comes on the Angel of Death says:

"You know, I like this version better than Dylan's."

I say "I do too."

And then the Angel of Death says "Levon Helm. So fucking great." The Angel of Death might be a little drunk.

I say "Yeah, so fucking great." I might be drunk too.

"Hey, I am going to take another whiz and be on my way."

I say "Let me grab you a paper towel."

"Thanks man."

The Angel of Death comes out of the bathroom singing "Any day now, any day now, I shall be released," smiles, then says "Thanks for the hang."

I say "My pleasure."

He says "I understand if you say no but any chance I can take the album. I am going to try and sneak it in."

I take the record off the turntable, slip it back into the sleeve and hand it to the him. A CD might be easier to hide but I am not about to argue with the Angel of Death. We say our goodbyes. I put the scotch glasses in the dishwasher.

Twenty minutes later I hear a knock

The Angel of Death is at my door.

"You going to the Greenberg wedding next week?"

I say "Yeah."

And he says "You might want to take an Uber."

THE FOURSOME

Photograph © Bruno Thethe / Unsplash

Allie called at 6:45 and told me she had a 7:17 spot available for me at Tutto Pronto. Most people might be offended to be asked at this late hour but Allie knows this is exactly how I like to have dinner. She also knows that although I am not a huge fan of public restaurants, Tutto is conveniently located five minutes from my house and has a delicious cacio e pepe pasta, which I love.

Also, I was starving.

I asked her who dropped out.

She said "Does it really matter?"

She was right. It didn't really matter.

I asked who else was in the foursome.

"Jeff and Becky," she replied.

I like Jeff and Becky. They are nice enough people. Not really nice enough to spend four hours dining with, but that is probably true about everyone else I know and if I adhered to that criteria I would likely always be dining alone.

No, the thing about Jeff and Becky is they are Allie's music friends, so the conversation invariably turns to music. Which would be perfectly fine if it was actually a conversation about music and did not turn into a digression about the quirks and shortcomings of the other people they play with.

Allie sensed my hesitation and said "We won't talk about music."

I said "Maybe we can just have drinks and appetizers?"

"No. Drinks, apps, dinner, and dessert."

I said "Ok. I will meet you there."

Seriously, the cacio e pepe is that good.

I walked over to Tutto and was there at 7:10. While it is always a crapshoot whether I actually show up, you can bank on the fact that if I do show up, I will be there on time.

Tutto was packed. That's the thing about these public restaurants - they get tons of traffic. There were two parties in front of me at the hostess desk. From the sounds of it, neither had reservations. That's right, 7:15 on a Saturday night. Just come right in without reservations. Are we at war?

When I got to the desk, the hostess, Jessica, smiled and said "It will be about a 45 minute to an hour wait."

I smiled back and said "Actually, I have a reservation. Allie for four." Allie is Allie's Starbucks name. It is her reservations name.

It is her name for these little stories. Sometimes I can't even remember her real name.

"Yes," answered Jessica, still smiling. "I see it here. Allie for 7:17. Is your entire party here?"

"It's not," I replied. I didn't want to get into an entire 'What difference does it make if my entire party is here' debate. Jessica was smiling but there was discernible anger lurking below. I didn't think I wanted to tangle with her.

"Okee dokee," she said. "Just let me know when you are all here."

"Ok."

"And," she looked down at her reservations sheet, "we are actually running about fifteen minutes behind. So you are now our 7:32."

Just then Allie walked up to the counter all out of breath, her dining shoes in her hands and not her feet, and announced "Allie. Table of 4 at 7:17."

"I'm standing right here," I said. "What do you think I was doing?"

"Nobody ever knows what you are doing," she replied. "Ignore him," she said to Jessica.

Jessica, whose smile had not wavered for five minutes straight, said "As I just told your," she nodded in my direction, "friend, we are running a little behind. You are now our 7:32."

"Why?" I said.

"Why what?"

"Why are you running behind?"

"Someone in the 6:45 group sent back their fillet. Said it was overdone."

"They sent back..."

Allie pulled me away from the counter. I sometimes got this way when I was hungry. Or even when I wasn't hungry.

"Did you skip lunch?"

"I'm fine," I said. "Fucking public restaurants. The place is a zoo."

"Anyway," she said, "it is a blessing in disguise. Jeff said he might be a little late."

"Jesus!"

"It's fine," she said in a voice which she thinks is soothing but I mostly find irritating, "let's go get a drink at the bar. You could probably use the practice." The bar was full. Most of the people had come just to practice eating. I hated to practice.

At 7:30, Becky texted Allie to say she was very sorry but they were going to have to cancel. Jeff wasn't feeling well. I went to go speak to Jessica.

"Jessica," I said, "our friends just cancelled. Any chance we can eat as a twosome?"

"It's Saturday night," she replied. "We really can't do twosomes."

"What if we started with dessert and worked backwards?"

"I'm sorry. No. We don't do that here. But I just had a cancellation. I can fit you in with the Johnsons at," she looked down at her sheet, "7:48. It's the next seating." Then she called out "Solvesborgs, your table is ready."

"Ok. Great. Thanks." I slinked back to the bar and told Allie. "7:48 with the Johnsons."

"Ok. That doesn't sound too bad."

"It does sound bad. It sounds very bad. And now we are behind the Solvesborgs."

"What is that supposed to mean?"

"Scandinavians," I whispered. "Notoriously slow eaters."

"Charming," she snorted.

"Let's just go order a pizza."

"No, we are here. It will be fun. Here, take a pretzel."

I was starving but wasn't about to eat a pretzel from a communal jar. I wasn't an animal.

Pouting might not be very mature but it did seem to make the time go faster. Next thing I knew Jessica was calling out "Johnson. Allie. Your table is ready."

We followed Jessica, her arms laden with four menus, to our table. But not before Jessica gently told me to tuck in my shirt. We passed a table of sturdy looking blonds I suspected were the Solvesborgs. Their table had drinks but no apps. This was going to get ugly.

The Johnsons were a lovely older couple from the other side of Avenue. The streets are a little narrower and the houses are a little more expensive. They were, we quickly learned within the first minute, both retired and now avid birders.

"I read recently that Leopold was an avid bird watcher," I said.

"Who?" Asked Mrs. Johnson, please call me Marjorie.

"Nathan Leopold. Of Leopold and Loeb. The murderers."

Most of the time I don't know why I say the things I do.

Allie kicked me under the table. This usually works. But this time it only slowed me down.

"Loeb was murdered in prison but Leopold eventually landed in Puerto Rico. He wrote the definitive book about birds from that island."

I wasn't trying to chase the Johnsons away. I was just trying to make conversation.

"Is this one of your regular restaurants?" Asked Allie, quickly changing the subject.

"It is," said Mr. Johnson. I'm sure he had told us his first name but I must have missed it thinking about my Leopold and Loeb story. "Marjorie loves their eggplant parm. What about you guys?"

"I love it here but this one," she elbowed me a little harder than needed, "he usually sticks to his private restaurants."

"Ah," smiled Mr. Johnson. I think it might have been either Bob or Bill. "So you're slumming it with us common folk tonight."

"No, no, not at all," I replied. "I really like this place. Their cacio e pepe is so good."

"Hey," said Marjorie, "that's Brian's favorite too!" Brian. Yes, Brian. Then she said, as god is my witness "Twinsies."

Our waitress, Colleen, said her name tag, came and asked if we wanted to order drinks.

"A bottle of red?" Suggested Brian.

"Maybe two," retorted Allie cheerily.

"Can we look at a wine list?" Asked Marjorie.

"Of course," said Colleen.

"And maybe a basket of bread?" I said. I was starving.

"Of course," replied Colleen. "I'll bring it the minute the table in front of you," she pointed at the Solvesborgs, "finishes theirs."

"They are so damn slow," I said. "Can we speed them up?"

Allie mouthed 'Take it easy' to me but it was going to be a bit of a struggle.

"Look at the way he is buttering his roll," I said to no one in particular. "An hour to butter a roll. Does he need butter on every exposed piece of bread? Just swipe a dab of it and take a bite for god's sake."

This time Allie did not mouth it. She said out loud "Take it easy."

I was very close to losing it but then Brian, god bless him, muttered something underneath his breath which brightened what had become an increasingly dark evening.

What he said was "Scandinavians."

Marjorie said "Oh Brian. You are terrible. Pay no attention to him. He has no manners."

I said "I know what you mean. They can be a little slow."

"Look," said Brian, "I'm all for enjoying a meal. Marj and I love to take our time. All I'm asking is for a little courtesy. We can't have our bread until they finish theirs. There has to be a limit."

"Amen," I said thumping the table. Then I signaled Colleen for another bottle of wine.

The bread basket was a salve for troubled times. I had two rolls and was reaching for a piece of olive oil sprinkled focaccia when Allie slapped my hand, muttering something about spoiling my appetite. We finished our bread but the Solvesborgs, now looking as pissed off as me, still didn't have their appetizers. I called Colleen over and asked her what the hold-up was. She said she would go check. She came back holding a basket of bread as a peace offering.

"The 7:15 group ordered a second batch of buffalo mozzarella," she said apologetically, "so we are running a tiny bit behind."

"There's nothing you can do?"

"Well if dinner runs longer than four hours and twelve minutes you will all get a free dessert coupon for next time."

"That buffalo mozzarella is good," said Allie. "I think I am going to order it."

"I feel bad about bad mouthing the Scandinavians," I said. "I didn't realize they were being held up.

Once I decided just to be zen and enjoy myself, we had a lovely time with the Johnsons. The cacio e pepe was as good as I remembered. I even shared a story about a yellow-bellied sapsucker which did not involve a murder. I sent over a bottle of wine to the Solvesborgs and told them to take their time.

The pace of eating was painfully slow. On a trip to the bathroom I passed a man on his hands and knees trying to retrieve a meatball which had rolled off the table. He was still at it when I returned. His eating partners looked embarrassed but did nothing to fix the situation. It makes me crazy when people don't adhere to the five-minute rule for lost food. Just get a new meatball for fucks sake!

Dinner was so slow that the Johnsons decided to take their leave shortly after their mains, eggplant parm and cacio e pepe, arrived. They didn't have time to have dessert.

As they got up to leave we saw that the Solvesborgs too had given up the ghost and decided to leave before dessert.

Allie and I, observing the traditional restaurant etiquette, cleaned up their plates and scooped up their crumbs. Colleen arrived with dessert menus and another twosome who were going to join us for dessert and coffee.

The Goodmans.

Jennifer and Bernard.

Jennifer declined Colleen's offer of a dessert menu.

"I only have the crème brûlée here," she declared. "Nothing else even comes close."

She sounded like she knew what she was talking about, so, with the coast now being totally clear, we ordered cappuccinos and four crème brûlées for the table.

We exchanged pleasantries as we waited for our coffee and dessert. Bernard was a semi-retired accountant and Jennifer was a former school teacher who said her passion was now gardening. I refrained from mentioning I had read Charles Manson was said to have had quite an impressive flower bed.

Bernard asked me what we did for a living. I explained that I too was semi-retired and was trying to reinvent myself as a writer.

"That's marvellous," exclaimed Jennifer. "Novels?"

"No," I replied. "Short stories. Humorous vignettes. That kind of thing."

Jennifer seemed a bit disappointed "Well that is writing too," she said. "You keep at it."

"Thank you," I said.

"Are you working on anything now?" Asked Bernard.

"Yes. I am almost finished this satire about the absurdity of golf. How we golfers put up with things we would never put up with in other parts of our lives. Imagine, for example, if dinner at a restaurant was like golf."

"Well, good luck with that," said Jennifer, who clearly thought I was nuts.

I started to explain but then someone in the back yelled out "FORE" and we all ducked under the table to avoid being hit by a wayward meatball.

JAFFA ORANGES

Photograph © SolStock / iStock

When I was twelve I was chosen to represent our Montreal suburb, Dollard-des-Ormeaux, for its under-13 soccer team.

Which is why, up until very recently, whenever the subject of soccer came up, there was a very good chance I would say, "You know, I played on a select team when I was young."

Select.

But this story is not about my soccer skills or about glory days.

It is about the lessons of history.

The biggest difference between playing in the house league and playing select soccer, outside of the quality of play, was that the house league was played at our local park, which was three blocks from our house, while the select games were played on soccer fields throughout Montreal and its suburbs. Places like Beaconsfield, Kirkland, Lake of Two Mountains, and Verdun.

It meant the fathers, it was always the fathers, of the players were responsible for carpooling the kids on Sunday mornings. They split up the shifts and it worked out to something like once every three weeks.

My father took his obligatory turn and loaded me and three of my teammates into his brown 1970 Chevy Impala. Once at the soccer field he would set up a small folding lawn chair under a shade tree and read his book, usually a volume of history, until the game ended. He would look up, bemused, if he heard a loud cheer and even once returned my wave when I ran by.

At the end of the game, he would respectfully, even a little solemnly shake coach McPherson's hand, as if they had just reached an accord on an arms treaty, pile the same crew into the Chevy, and drop them off at their respective homes.

He would ask me if it was good - c'était bien? - never if we had won, and I would then give him a quick recap. He was a big believer in physical fitness and I think he was pleased to see me running outside in the fresh air, but the concept of winning and losing was not one he deemed worthy of his attention. I know he played basketball when he was young but I had never seen him watch or talk about sports. When the newspaper arrived, he handed me the sports section.

I found the entire ordeal more than a bit stressful. Besides the lawn chair, the book, the sometimes socks with sandals, my father drove painfully slow - the Chevy had never once visited the passing lane - and he insisted on playing classical music the entire time. I begged him to play pop music or no music at all but the conversation was a nonstarter. The best compromise I could come up with was he would not turn up the volume for the canons during the 1812 Overture. He did enjoy taking us to Dairy Queen though, he loved his ice cream, and that would usually help temper the embarrassment of the slow driving and the Tchaikovsky unless one of my teammates made the mistake of getting into the car with an unfinished cone still dripping in his hand. He wouldn't say anything. Just slowly and sternly wag his finger no. My father was a tall man who had played basketball as a teen. Years later, NBA star Dikembe Mutombo had a trade mark 'not in my house' finger wag when swatting away balls headed for the basket. My friend Steve Kahansky, who had been on the receiving end of my father's finger wags plenty of times, would always say that Dikembe stole it from Marco Zevy.

All in all I managed to survive carpooling and it had been a great summer, until the Sunday when it was our turn to be in charge of the other team obligation: providing the halftime oranges.

In theory, it should have been a very simple task. Fill a cooler with ice. Cut the oranges. Put the oranges in the cooler.

We had a cooler.

We had ice.

We had oranges.

Well, we did have oranges. But we didn't have the oranges everyone else had. They had California navel oranges. It is the most eaten orange in North America. Readily available in any and every supermarket. But the Zevys didn't have California navel oranges. No. We had Israeli Jaffa oranges.

Could we maybe get regular oranges I wondered out loud.

Jaffa oranges, my father proclaimed, are the best oranges in the entire world. Your team is in for a treat.

He was not wrong. Jaffa oranges were delicious. But I was just trying to fit in. And I would have argued a little bit more to get my way if I didn't have to deal with another, more pressing, issue.

My father refused to leave the peels on.

From week one, all the oranges were cut in four, with the peels intact. At halftime, the players would grab a slice or two and suck on them. Then discard the peels, as the juice ran down their chins, into a big green garbage bag. That's how we did it. Every week. Every single week. But now my father wanted to remove the peels of the oranges, the Jaffa oranges, and offer up peel-free slices.

I asked him why.

He shrugged his shoulders and then answered in English. It was a language he spoke fluently. One of the seven languages he spoke. But it was a language he never ever spoke with his children, fearing, presciently, they would forget how to speak French, their mother tongue.

He said "Because we are not animals." He then handed me a knife and I stood next to him at the kitchen counter, removing peels, making slices, and putting them into plastic bags.

The score was 1-0 for our opponents at halftime when Coach McPherson asked me to go fetch my father. We had started eating the oranges and nobody had said a word about the type of oranges or the fact that they had no peels but my heart was still pounding as I went to get my father. He was reading a Churchill biography. I told him the coach wanted to speak with him. He placed a bookmark in the book, dog earing was for heathens, got up and followed me back to the team bench.

Coach McPherson said "Mr. Zeevy, I've got a wee bit of a family emergency. I wonder if you could coach the lads for the second half."

I have no idea why Coach McPherson asked my father. He had never expressed an interest in soccer. Had never even watched more than a minute of a game. The other fathers knew the game. They knew the team. They knew the players. But maybe those solemn handshakes had made an impression. I was hoping, praying, he would just bow out and let one of the others take the helm, but my father had a strong sense of duty and always doing the right thing.

My father spoke English fluently. Still, it was always strange to hear him in English. Unlike my Uncle Henri, whose English sounded like the late Egyptian president Anwar Sadat, my father's accent, although undeniable, was harder to place. Like a wine tasting, you could detect hints and bouquets of Cairo, of Jerusalem, of Paris, of remote and exotic towns and villages. He now addressed me and my teammates in that accented English. Using a stick he had picked up from the ground, he began to make scratchings in the dirt. If I had a stick I would have made a hole big enough to crawl into. He did not know anybody's name so he just pointed and said "You". As in "You go here." "You go there." It was a very offensive and aggressive 2-3-5 alignment. Completely different than the way we usually played. He didn't speak again in the half other than to make substitutions. He made sure everyone played. We scored three goals and won easily.

We didn't speak after the game. Together we carried the cooler, it had leftover oranges because we had brought too much, back to the car. We went back home. He drove as slowly as ever, played Mozart at a low volume, and we even stopped for our regular Dairy Queen.

My mother greeted us at the door and asked how the game was.

I said "We won 3-1!" Then, pointing at my father excitedly, said "He was our coach!"

She looked up at my father with a surprised look and asked what I had wanted to ask.

"What do you know about soccer?"

He shrugged his shoulders and, still speaking English, said:

"The 1956 Hungarian national team. The Magyar formation."

Then he walked into the house wearing his socks and sandals and carrying his Churchill biography.

CAESAR SALAD

Photograph © Vadym Drobot / Alamy

I am down on the dock at the cottage with Danna and her friend Sally and they are trading blind date war stories. It really is a bit of a joke.

To begin with, 'blind' is such a misnomer that it is laughable. This generation has seen more pictures of their prospective dates than I have of my entire family collectively. When we went in blind, we really went in blind. Armed with no more, especially if the set up was from a female friend, than weathered adjectives about bubbly personalities and shared interests, and creatively ambitious promises about looks. "She looks a lot like Demi Moore," the wife might say while her husband bit his lip and stared downward at a fascinating piece of grass. I suspect tall tales were also told about me. I went on a lot of blind dates with women who, upon opening the front door, were completely unable to mask their disappointment. I saw a lot of the "Oh socks, I really needed socks" Christmas present look. A date most surely over before it had even begun, but now there would be two hours of forced conversation, "Do you like to travel? I love to travel", over plates of baked salmon and asparagus to look forward to. Then a perfunctory follow up phone call two days later in the quixotic hope that you completely misread the situation and that her look of only slightly contained nausea was in fact just one of concealed excitement.

These kids today have no clue. Nor any inkling of grammar or vocabulary. No need for a crack forensic team to decode a message on an answering machine.

Now they have emojis.

An emoji which takes care of sending a direct and unambiguous message about every situation. Should you be ambitious and take advantage of the richness of the English language, you might write 's'up.' Or, really dig deep into the well of words and type out a real tome - 'Netflix and chill.' Complete words and sentences are becoming rarer than a lunar eclipse.

"Now if I had access to text back in the day," I mused out loud.

I was not saying I could have done better. I was just saying I could not have done worse.

Danna's friend Sally, she actually does look a little like Demi Moore, asks if I have any blind date stories, and Danna rolls her eyes and says "He has a whole book of them." Which is true. I have written plenty of stories about blind dates.

"Tell the Caesar salad story," says Danna.

"It's a blind date story?" Asks Sally.

"Yes," chimes in Danna. "It is epic. Tell her who set you up."

I had forgotten about that. The phone number had come from my Tante Odette in Montreal. She called me every week for two months. I finally relented on week 9.

"Tonto," I say, referring to the nickname my family and all our friends call her.

"Tonto!" Says Sally who, having been friends with Danna since grade school, has an intimate knowledge of all of the members of our whacky family. "Oh, this is going to be good.

I get up and help myself to a couple of clementines from a bowl we have been sharing, cavalierly throwing the rinds into the trees behind us, assuming they are biodegradable. I return to my chair but not before first dragging it to a lonely square of shade I have found precariously close to the end of the dock

I toss a clementine to Sally. She and Danna, unlike me, have angled their lounge chairs in order to get the most of the late afternoon sun.

"Actually, the shocking part is that it was a good set up. Tonto played cards with a woman whose niece had just moved to Toronto."

"So you called her?"

"Yeah. But you have to understand it wasn't so straight forward. You had to find a good time to call and you couldn't just leave a message on the answering machine."

"Why not?"

"It just wasn't done. The first call had to be live. I think I hung up five times on the machine before I got through to her."

"That is jokes."

"No. What is jokes is she had never heard of me. She had no idea I was going to call. It took fifteen minutes before we could figure out the connection. I was surprised she even agreed to go out with me."

"Classic Tonto," says Danna.

"Why is it called the Caesar salad story?" Asks Sally.

I smile and answer.

"We went out for dinner and she ordered Caesar salad for an appetizer and Caesar salad with chicken as her main."

"Seriously?" Asks Sally.

"Yes," I reply.

"That's a true story?"

"Yup."

"That's a lot of garlic," says Sally. "Are you sure she wasn't trying to tell you something?"

"Maybe. But she went out with me twice more."

"The story gets better," pipes in Danna.

It is true. The story is much longer. But I don't like to tell it.

I suppose there are only so many stories but we writers always want to think we are coming up with something new and clever. Sometimes I choose not to tell a story, or at least not include it in a collection, because it seems a little too derivative. That is true of the Caesar salad story because the longer version is actually the 'the time I forgot my date's name' story and it sounds all too much like the classic Seinfeld 'Mulva' episode. I think it is a pretty good story and is really, beyond the forgetting of the name, really nothing like the 'Mulva' episode, but on occasion, when I tell it, someone will say "Oh, just like the Seinfeld episode," or worse, "Did you base that on the Seinfeld episode?"

And I don't really want to explain why it is different because the story is kind of ruined by then.

"This I gotta hear," says Sally.

So I tell the rest of the story.

Now I don't know how old I was when this happened but it doesn't really matter because there was never a time when I wasn't childish, immature, and juvenile and there was never a time when I didn't surround myself with friends who were also childish, immature and juvenile. And because we, Allie, Lewberg, Goldfarb, and I were childish, immature and juvenile, during the days between date one and date two and the days between date two and date three, we didn't call this woman by her given name.

Instead we called her Caesar salad.

As in "Where are you taking Caesar salad?"

Or:

"What time are you picking up Caesar salad?"

This woman, whose name will most assuredly come to me before I get to the end of this story, came to her nickname honestly. She ordered Caesar salad all three times we went out.

"Once at a Chinese restaurant," says Danna, stealing the thunder of my mid-story joke. It isn't true, of course. It is a fictional detail which found its way into the story and, as it does here, usually gets a big laugh and so earned its place in subsequent telling. It is a little unfair because, other than her unusual penchant for Caesar salad, she was funny, attractive, and very nice.

Date three was at the Dip on College Street. I didn't tell Lewberg, Goldfarb, or Allie where I was taking Caesar salad on our third date because I didn't put it past any of them to come snooping by, so it was likely a complete coincidence, although the patio at Cafe Diplomatico was one of my go-to places, when Lewberg suddenly appeared on College Street making his way to the corner of Clinton where she and I were sitting.

He was about fifteen feet away when I realized I had forgotten her actual name. We had used her nickname so often it had become lodged in my brain. Which sent me into an understandable panic.

When Lewberg got to our table, smiling at his good fortune for having discovered us, I looked up at him and said, mind you, to someone I had known for most of my adult life, "I'm terribly embarrassed but I have forgotten your name."

And Lewberg, unfazed or perhaps bolstered, by the number of Kettle and crans he had already consumed that night, had the good sense to stick out his hand and say "Lewberg. Nice to meet you."

Then she shook his hand and said "Sandra, so nice to meet you."

Then I said "Oh right, Lewberg. Of course, Lewberg. I am so sorry."

But what I meant to say was:

"Oh Right. Sandra. Sandra. Sandra. Not Caesar salad."

Then Lewberg, who is as solid a wing man as one could ask for, declined my offer to join us. Which may have been the one and only time he has ever turned down a drink.

"I love that part Uncle Ronnie," says Danna. "I have to give you credit. That was pretty smart."

"Yes," agrees Sally. "That was a baller move. Then what happened?"

"We went back to my apartment."

That's what we did. We went back to my apartment. I excused myself and went to the bathroom. I left Sandra in the living room where I had a fireplace. The fireplace had a wide mantle.

I don't keep that many pictures on my mantle. I have a few of my parents, my brother, my sister, my nephews and nieces. There is a picture of Sammy and I when I published No Nuts for Me. And a really nice group one from Pebble Beach from the time I got my hole in one.

Four of us.

The Pacific Ocean in the background.

Me.

Avram Kashitsky.

Goldfarb.

and Lewberg.

Lewberg.

That was the picture Sandra was holding in her hand when I came out of the bathroom in my apartment.

"Isn't that Lewberg?" She said.

"Omg!" Says Sally. "No way."

I say "Way."

"I guess you didn't go out with her again."

"Nope."

"Great story," she says. She gets up and heaves the clementine rinds into the trees then nudges the lounge chair with her knee in order to better greet the sun. My shade has shifted but I am too lazy to move my chair. Anyway, the sun feels good and the three of us soak it up without speaking.

And then Sally breaks the silence "You know," she says, "it kinda reminds me of that Seinfeld episode."

THE THEORY OF RELATIVITY

Photograph © Keystone-France/Gamma-Keystone via Getty Images

I have a new girl-friend. We have been having quite a lot of sex.

Right there. That's the story.

I sometimes have the tendency to prattle on and on. I veer off and take long and unnecessary excursions from the main story line. Then invariably, I go back and delete large sections of the piece in order to make it concise and precise. But not this time. This time I am going to anticipate those changes and take a pre-emptive strike. No more digressions. Just straight and to the point.

I have a new girl-friend. We have been having quite a lot of sex.
The End

I admire my handiwork. Very solid opening line. Not surprising. Opening lines are kind of my jam. And the closer, the last line, is a thing of beauty. It's my signature move. I circle back and wrap the story up in one big beautiful bow. I think it's good. I think it is very good. I read it again to see if there is something I have missed. Sometimes, I get a little bolt of inspiration during the fourth or fifth reading.

I have a new girl-friend. We have been having quite a lot of sex.
The End

I like it.

I send it to Miles. Miles nominally is an employee for my company, but mostly he just edits my stories. What I will do is copy the story from my iPhone and then paste it into our Skype conversation. I can see by the green dot he is online and sure enough, I am soon seeing the tell-tale signs of a message coming back to me.

'Nice!!'

Miles has pretty good instincts and despite the fact he works for me he does not shy away from telling me if a piece doesn't work. Two exclamation marks. That's a good sign although I am pretty confident about this story.

I say thanks and ask him to clean it up and send it back to me. It means he will clean up the typos and grammar and also space it out properly. A few times, he took some liberties and changed up a word or two but I sent it back with my original copy so he doesn't do that anymore.

He emails it back to me with a fix and a note - girlfriend is not hyphenated - and then I forward it to Jules.

Jules writes back right away and says thanks for the new piece and he will try to get to it this weekend. Now I have to wait. Jules will tell me if it is good enough for the new collection. Or, if it is not that great, he will tell me it is a piece my friends and family will enjoy.

In the meantime, I send it to the regular cast of characters for their feedback and reactions. I also send it to Helen who is our book designer and responsible for laying out both the Amazon kindle and the paperback version. Plus, she will find or create a photo to accompany the story.

Lewberg is the first to write back. He texts "Epic. Love the ending. Top ten in my books." Good old Lewberg. I can always count on him for some positive feedback.

Tatiana is next "OMG. Hilarious!!!"

Now the story wasn't really meant to be funny but I guess it could be. I read it again.

I have a new girlfriend. We have been having quite a lot of sex. The End

Yeah. Yeah. I could see how that could be funny. I am kind of proud of myself. I am evolving as a writer. Putting together pieces which can be appreciated on many levels. Nice!

Allie chimes in next. "I lurve it." I discount all of Allie's feedback. I could send her a grocery list and she would tell me she loved it.

I am surprised to hear back from Goldfarb though. I send him all of my stories and he never responds. Even for a book filled with stories about him. He's not a fan of my writing.

I pick up the phone.

"A lot of sex?" He says.

He is not wrong. I may have taken some creative license with my description.

"A lot for me," I reply.

"Anything more than 0 is a lot for you."

Goldfarb is not trying to stick it to me. He's just trying to be factual.

Then I say "Well, like Einstein said, it's all relative."

Goldfarb says "Einstein's theory of relativity was about gravity not the number of times you have sex you moron."

I should know better than to mention Einstein in front of Goldfarb. I try to explain, but he has already hung up.

My friend Harold writes back. "I am not really a fan of science fiction." There is no happy face emoji.

I then hear from my friend Walshy. She is a writer and has been very supportive.

"Have been having' is a little clunky," she says.

"Hmm. You think?" I say it in my head. Have been having. Yeah, it does sound a little clunky. I really trust and respect Walshy's opinion.

"What do you suggest?" I ask.

"You can try 'we are having'" she says. "It changes it into the present tense and avoids the clunkiness. You kill two birds with one stone."

I say. "Ok thanks."

So I change it.

I have a new girlfriend. We are having quite a lot of sex.
The End

Yes, she is right. It is better that way. I now resend it to Miles and to Jules and to Helen. I mark it version 2.

I then hear from my friend Faye. She is a strict grammarian.

"Great story," she says.

I can see a dot dot dot.

I know a 'but' is coming.

"But I'm not crazy about the modifier."

"The modifier?"

"Quite. Quite a lot of sex. It doesn't add anything to the sentence. It is superfluous."

Hmm. I hadn't thought of that. I try both in my head. We are having quite a lot of sex. We are having a lot of sex. I think I liked it better my way. I decide to push back.

"It's stylistic," I argue. "It is a little garnish. Like capers."

"Nobody likes or needs capers," she says. "It is just an extra word."

"Ok. Thanks. Let me sleep on it."

"Also..."

"Yes?"

"'Have been having' is a little clunky."

I say "Way ahead of you."

But I don't sleep on it. I bang around the house obsessing about it and then decide Faye is right. It is hard to lose a word. But sometimes you have to cut in order to let the rest of the garden grow. I try it the new way.

I have a new girlfriend. We are having a lot of sex.
The End

Ugh. I hate being wrong. But it is better. I have to admit it is better. I send version 3 to Miles, Jules and Helen.

Then Allie calls.

"I lurve the new story," she says.

"Thanks," I reply. I made a few edits since you last read it. I think it is even better."

"I thought it was great as it was." Allie is always so supportive. "What did Hannah think?"

"Who?"

"Hannah. The aforementioned new girlfriend."

"Oh. Right. I haven't shown it to her yet. She says she prefers to read the stories in an actual book. She is going to wait for the paperback to come out."

"How is she going to feel when she reads you have been writing about how much sex you are having?"

I hadn't really thought of that. All of my other stories have been about previous girlfriends. I have never written a story about a current girlfriend. I was just so caught up in the story.

"Damn!" I say. "I didn't really think it through."

"I don't think you will be having any sex if she reads that sentence."

"You think?"

"I know. You have to get rid of it."

"Get rid of it? But it's my all-time favorite sentence. It ties the whole story together."

"Not sure what to tell you. Unless you want to change it to 'ex-girlfriend'. Besides, I think the story works without it."

"You're just saying that."

"I think it holds up. Give it a try."

So I do.

I have a new girlfriend.
The End

I mean, it is good. It is a perfectly good story. But, it makes me sick to know what it could have been. I send version 4 to Miles, Jules, and Helen.

On Monday I hear back from Jules.

"I enjoyed your piece. While it has many of the literary flourishes which usually adorn your work it somehow feels a little unfocussed. I think it is almost there. You may want to sit on it for a year or two and let it breath. Also, and I hope I am not sounding like a broken record, but I think it is a little too long.

BIRDWATCHING

Photograph by Orly

Claire asks if I have any sunscreen. We have driven two and half hours in traffic on a Saturday morning in order to spend the day - I have only agreed to drive up on the condition that I don't have to spend the night - at her friends Todd and Jenna's cottage in the Kawarthas. We have stopped twice. Once to buy blueberry pie and once to buy corn. The pie place had corn but it was not, Claire made clear, the kind of corn we wanted. Then I had to pee and suggested we stop one more time at the gas station but Claire said the cottage is only fifteen minutes away. And it would have been, had Todd given us decent directions. Instead we take a route which lands us on their circular driveway 45 minutes later.

Which is only to say that when Claire asks if I have sunscreen I am in a bit of a state and answer without thinking it through. So I say "There's a tube of Coppertone SPF 30 in my golf bag." And there is. A brand-new tube. Right in the outside pouch where I keep my golf gloves. It is also, I realize a few seconds too late, where I keep my binoculars. Which Claire now has in her hands.

"What is this??

It is a pair of Zeis Conquest HD binoculars which I have recently upgraded to.

I look her straight in the eye and say "I have been spying on this couple copulating on the 1st floor of the building across from our condo."

But that was a lie.

And Claire knows that was a lie.

I have been bird watching.

Ordinarily, I would wave off complaints about my various peccadillos, neuroses, obsessions, and phobias by saying she knew exactly what she was getting into. Which didn't really ever make her any less mad or frustrated but at least it gave me a slightly elevated perch, even if it were as precarious as Hillary's Step, nearer to the moral high ground.

But this time I do not have much of a leg to stand on. This is not what she signed up for.

It had started with the stamp collecting. She was not crazy about the stamp collecting. Especially since I had taken it up two months after we started dating. She didn't like the sight of torn off envelopes soaking in my orange popcorn bowl in the middle of the dining room table. She didn't like my stamp albums strewn all over the couch. She didn't like my silver tweezers. She didn't like my magnifying glass. She didn't like having to wait an extra twenty minutes to start a show we were binging because I had my nose buried in a catalogue of Olympic stamps from Cambodia. But she especially didn't like dating a guy who collected stamps.

"His father collected stamps," she would say apologetically when I hauled out my tall ship themed stamp albums for guests to peruse with their coffee and crème brûlée after dinner. It wasn't a hobby. It was a genetic defect.

I couldn't really blame her. Nobody collected stamps any more. It was something you did when you were ten. Not a hobby you picked up at sixty. She didn't know what to make of it. I mean, I guessed if I was otherwise normal it might be ok. But, as I am often reminded by friends and family, I am not.

I liked collecting stamps. I liked the history. I liked the geography. I liked the designs. I found it relaxing and even, dare I say, interesting.

Then I started up with coins. Nothing crazy. Just a couple of antique Roman and Greek coins. Some cool Canadian silver dollars. Ok, maybe the occasional gold commemorative. But really, nothing big. A handful of coins. Not even a collection. Unlike the stamps, I could keep them in my pocket. I liked to reach in and jingle them. Sometimes I jangled them. I paid a pretty penny for a 70AD antique Hebrew coin which was minted to fund the Bar Kochba revolt against the Romans. From 70AD!!

I mean how cool is that!

Claire liked the coins even less than the stamps. Not only was it nerdy. It was, what was the word she used... smarmy.

"Smarmy? Are you sure you even know what that means?" I argued. "Maybe it isn't smarmy," she relented. "It just feels, you know, unsavory." It felt so old. So uncool. But despite her protestations - when we left the house she would say "No stamps no coins" - she remained a good sport about it. In fact, she even bought me a set of Ottoman Empire circa 1800 coins for my birthday. Claire was a good egg. But, to her, it kind of felt like a bait and switch. She had already agreed to golf and poker. She had initialed the contract. She wanted to be in a relationship which didn't keep adding addendums.

But we sorted it out. We compromised. We settled it. I liked her. I liked her more than I am letting on. I knew I was lucky to have her.

Then came the birds.

Here's the thing. The internet has taken a little mystique out of collecting stamps and coins. Because everything is available. You aren't really collecting. You are acquiring. Your collection can be as big as your bank account allows. There doesn't seem to be any sport or skill to it.

But you can't really buy birds. Sure, you could get on a plane and travel to an exotic locale. You could be part of a listserv which alerts you to a sighting. But you can't add a bird to a shopping cart. You can't build your life list by going to Amazon. Unless it is the actual Amazon. You have to go out and see it. Birders call it 'getting' a bird. Also, the entire hobby is based on the honor system. Birders are just as likely to boast about birds they had missed as they were about birds they had 'gotten'.

I knew birding would put her over the top. She had joked about it when disparaging my other hobbies. "At least it isn't birdwatching," she had sighed to Jenna one night. Camels and their backs would require a team of spine surgeons.

Claire was not alone in warning me to stay away. When I mentioned my interest in front of my family, my niece Danna, shook her head and said "That's a hard no, Uncle Ronnie. I just don't think you can afford to get any weirder. You really have no margin for error."

"I think it could be fun," I replied, unconvinced.

"It won't be fun for us. You are going to start posting blurry pictures of birds in our group chat. Then you will get pissed off if we don't like them. Can't you just collect stamps with pictures of birds on them?"

I didn't tell her I already had a full album of bird themed stamps. It wasn't doing it for me.

Allie was no more supportive.

"Claire will not be happy," she said. Allie was not a huge Claire fan but still thought it was unwise.

"Can you birdwatch ironically?" She joked. I didn't think so. Anyway, I was sure to hate it. I didn't like early mornings. I didn't like periods standing outside. I didn't like rain. I wasn't that crazy about nature. I didn't really even like people. I wasn't sure I even liked birds. I still list Hitchcock's avian oeuvre as the scariest movie I have ever seen. On the other hand, as a Florida winter migrator myself, it was hard not to marvel at the majesty of the egret, the aerodynamically defiant swoop of the red hawk, and the surreal otherworldliness of an actual pink flamingo. In general, I liked reading about things much more than doing them. Why start an argument which would be moot in a week? I was just going to dip my toe and then go back to my life.

So I found a local group and sent an email to the coordinator, Tammy Levitan Shore, and asked if they would allow a newbie to tag along. Sure, she said. The more the merrier. Sunday morning. 7am. Was there a later minyan I asked? 7:10 was allowed but you had better come with a tray full of Tim Horton's. 7:00am was uncivilized. But I would go once and then be done with it. I just wanted to see if it was going to be as bad as I thought. I called Lewberg and told him to cover for me. I was going to tell Claire I was golfing if she asked.

"Please tell me you are getting some action on the side," said Lewberg.

"I'm going birdwatching," I said.

"Please tell me that is a euphemism for getting some action on the side."

"I'm going birdwatching," I repeated.

"It's not easy being your friend," said Lewberg. Then he hung up.

I got to the parking lot of Earl Bales park at 6:45 with two dozen chocolate glazed donuts.

It was not, technically speaking, the first time I had gone bird watching - I had accompanied my friends Jeff and Orly a couple of times on short jaunts on the boardwalk which ran through a wetland preservation park not far from my home in Boca. But I had gone mostly for the walk, the company, and the chance of seeing an alligator. Jeff, a birder by marriage, impressed me with his identification prowess. From time to time, Orly, a remarkably talented amateur photographer, would send me pictures she had taken. Once, she had sent me a picture of the Bugs Bunny themed yellow-bellied sapsucker. But this would be the first time I had gone with the express purpose of looking at birds.

The members of the North York Easy Birding Society shuffled in minutes later. I had calculated perfectly. Twelve of us set off at exactly 7:00 am. Two donuts per person. Not a single person arrived late.

It was a Hollywood version of a motley crew.

I was, at 61, the youngest person.

I was the only one without binoculars.

I was the only one not wearing a bird-themed shirt or hat.

I was the only person who was not really, really cheerful.

I was, it became apparent after we crested the first hill, in the worse shape.

The other thing which became clear within the first hour is that my eyes did not appear to work. The childhood ditty taunted me. I had brought my specs but my eyes were still dim and I could not see.

Tammy Levitan Shore, a retired civil litigation lawyer, took it upon herself to walk by my side, loan me her back up pair of binoculars, and point out examples of some of the 300 different types of bird species native to Toronto which graced our presence that morning. The only thing was, I couldn't see any birds. There were trees, there were branches, there were leaves. There was a good bit of rustling. Also, bird-like noises, I guess you could say IRL tweets, which all sounded identical to me. But no sightings.

Tammy Levitan Shore, on the other hand, could not stop seeing birds.

A Cardinal

A Downy woodpecker

A Song sparrow

A Nuthatch

A Black capped chickadee

Bless her heart, every sighting was if it were her first.

She would nudge me gently and point at a branch. I would then bring the binocular to my face and try, in vain, to find it.

Oh yes, I said. I see it.

Birdwatching is based on the honor system. I had been out there for less than twenty minutes and was already lying through my teeth. I had also quickly developed a crick in my neck. I didn't mind the walk. I didn't mind being out here in the woods. But at least now I knew this is not for me. I spent the next two hours pleasantly nodding my head and making small talk about things I knew nothing about.

And then I saw the owl.

I saw it because I had to pee. We had been out here for a couple of hours and I hadn't seen any of the other men - we were divided equally - sidle up to a tree to relieve themselves. I didn't know what the protocol was. I didn't know if the forest was considered sacred ground which I should not desecrate. But I had to pee. So I separated myself from the rest and zig zagged through the path in order to find a private spot. I was zipping up when I saw the owl. I was five feet away. At ten feet, I wouldn't have noticed it. Later, I learned it was a barred owl. It was a good get. I surreptitiously snapped a picture but the owl couldn't give a shit. It wasn't moving. Then it did that thing I had seen on TV where it rotates its neck like a spring action toy. I would have stared a little while longer but I heard someone call my name so I sprinted back.

The thing about birders is they are very generous. They get a bird and they want you to get it too. The book, The Big Year, which was later made into a so-so movie with Jack Black, is about a cut-throat competition to amass the most sightings in one year. But that wasn't my experience. My experience was that birders are great sharers. But I didn't share my barred owl. I kept that one for myself. In the next few months I got a few more birds on my own. My eyes got a little better and the binoculars began to make a difference once I knew what I was looking for. I didn't really get totally into it but I liked to dabble.

Claire adopted a don't ask don't tell policy. I no longer tell her I am golfing and she doesn't ask where I am going. I walk outside and become a bit more aware of my surroundings. The birds, it goes without saying, have been there all along. Of course, it takes me three days to notice Claire has cut her hair. But that's another story.

Todd and Jenna are excited to see us. They have a list of possible activities. Do we want to go on a boat ride, a swim, a hike, or just veg on the dock first? Claire thinks a hike followed by a swim. It sounds good to me. Jenna says they have found an amazing hike. She says she will get snacks and water bottles. I go in and find a bathroom. When I come back they are ready to go.

Claire smiles at me and says "Go on. Go get them."

I hesitate.

Then she turns to Todd and Jenn and says "This one has turned into a birdwatcher. He has binoculars in the car."

I don't correct her and say that the approved nomenclature is birder. Her mentioning it at all is a huge step.

I walk backwards to the car and retrieve the binoculars, wondering if this is just a prank.

But no. It really is a thing.

Jenna says. "Birdwatching eh. I love that for you."

Todd says "Dude, you are in for a treat. A lot of great birds on this hike."

He is right. On the way back I snap off five or six pictures of a great blue heron. It is a beauty.

I post the best shot on our family group chat.

I get no likes.

About five hours later Danna posts "Nice. Get a life Uncle Ronnie."

But I already have.

THE CONDOLENCE

Please accept my condolences for your loss.

Lewberg sent me a text.

"Alex's father passed away. RIP."

I wrote back and said thanks for letting me know.

Alex Fishman is a guy I know from a poker game I used to play in a few years ago. It wasn't my regular poker game. It was Lewberg's with guys he knew from work and golf. I sometimes filled in when they were short. I liked the game. Nice guys. Good food. Quality of poker was not great but the banter was pretty good and the guys had always been welcoming. I didn't know Alex that well. No more or less than the other guys. Poker nights was the only time I ever saw them and, like I said, I was just a part time fill in. I hadn't played in two or three years. It would have been the last time I had seen Alex Fishman. He wasn't a friend and barely an acquaintance.

But both of my parents had passed away and although I never found the week of shiva all that comforting, I did really appreciate the calls, emails and texts. Sometimes it was from people who were no longer really a part of my life but, the end of the day, it was just a nice thing to do and it was appreciated. It took all of two minutes. So now, I did my best to send timely and sincere condolences. Better to do it sooner than later. Also, it was easy to convince yourself a text was the better approach because the mourners were being inundated with calls and had to constantly tell the same story over and over again. Anyway, that's what I convinced myself. I still had Alex's phone number in my contact list so I crafted a short 'please accept my condolences for your loss' and sent it off. I had never met his father. Had never heard any stories about his father. I guess I would go to the shiva one night with Lewberg. Hopefully they would have a minyan. And that would be that.

The next day I received a text from Lewberg

"Fishman's father just dropped dead of a heart attack on the fourteenth green at Oakdale"

I texted back "Lewberg. You already told me this yesterday. Maybe lay off the Kettle and cranberry in the middle of the day"

There was no reply from Lewberg. I was about to put my phone away when I saw the telltale dot dot dot of an incoming text. Then it stopped. Then it started again. Then it stopped. Either Lewberg was writing a hella long text or he was writing, changing his mind, erasing, then writing again.

Finally the text came through.

"Please tell me you didn't already send out a condolence."

"I did. Five minutes after you told me. I don't dilly dally. Why?"

"Call me right now!"

I called him. He answered on the first ring.

"Alexandra Soffer." He said.

Alexandra Soffer was Lewberg's high school girlfriend.

"Yeah. What about her?"

"Alexandra. Alex. Alex. Her father died yesterday. He was 97."

I said "I don't understand." But I did.

"Alex is Alexandra. Alexandra is Alex. Fishman is Fishman. Fishman is not Alex. He is Fishman.

He was, of course right. Fishman was Fishman. We never called him Alex. I just figured Lewberg called him Alex because his father had just died. The only other Alex we had in common was Alexandra Soffer. We used to hang out a lot. Even go out on double dates. I had been to her house and to her cottage. But I had not thought of her in 20 years.

I hadn't sent condolences.

I had just predicted a man's death.

I call Allie.

I say "I have a situation."

As usual, she replies "Your life is a situation."

I ignore her.

"Alex Fishman's father died of a heart attack on the 14th hole at Oakdale today."

"That is horrible," she replied. "Who is Alex Fishman?"

"A guy I play poker with."

"Why does it matter it was on the fourteenth?"

"It doesn't."

"Was it a Zakarian heart attack? Did he get a hole in one?"

"No" Although I didn't know if it was.

"How old was he?"

"I don't know."

"When is the funeral?"

"I don't know."

"You should send your friend a condolence text or email."

"I did already. I sent him a text."

"Ok. Good."

"But here's the thing. I sent it to him yesterday."

"I don't understand."

"He didn't die yesterday. He died today."

I explained her the Alex and Alexandra and Fishman thing.

She said "hmmm." Then she said "You've got yourself a situation."

"I feel sick."

"It was an honest mistake. Just text him and explain. He will probably get dozens and dozens of texts. Yours will just get lost in a long list."

So I write it up. It is a bit longer than it should be. I say sorry or very sorry seven different times. I check three times to make sure I am sending it to Fishman. Then send. I feel sick about it. I don't sleep a wink all night.

Two days later, I am at Elijah Fishman's funeral at the Beth Tzeddeck Synagogue with Lewberg and some of the other poker guys. The place is packed. Many grandchildren get up and tell wonderful and heartwarming tales about their Zaida. There is a lot of sniffling. There is quite a bit of crying. Then Alex Fishman gets up. Lewberg and I are sitting in the back but we can tell he has been crying too. I think I might throw up. Alex tells the story of his father. How he fought in Israel's war of independence. How he got married and raised his family in Canada. It is the irony of funerals that you learn more about the man when he is dead than when he was arrive. It is a beautiful speech. About halfway through, my phone begins to vibrate. I reach into my suit breast pocket and pull out the phone so I can turn it off. But I take a quick peek first to see who the text is from.

It is from Alex Fishman.

Who, at this moment is still in the middle of his eulogy.

Lewberg, not exactly the master of social graces, elbows me in my shoulder. "Not cool man." He says.

I move the phone over to him so he can see what I have just read.

"While I very much appreciate your kind words, my father is very much alive and kicking. I don't know who this Alex character is but he hasn't done a very good job of telling people his number has changed. This isn't the first text I have received. So you may want to tell him. Also, send my condolences."

Alex Fishman is hitting the high emotional notes in his eulogy. Many people are sobbing loudly. I pinch myself as hard as I can to keep from smiling.

KASHKAVAL

Rabbi Jose the Galilean did not look happy. It was the morning before the first night of Passover and I was in Ararat, the Armenian deli a few blocks from my house, in order to pick up a slab of Bulgarian kashkaval cheese, some kalamata olives, and a jar of blackberry jam from Georgia. The Georgia with the hard to pronounce capital of Tbilisi.

Passover, the week-long holiday celebrating the Jewish exodus from slavery in Egypt, was the most observed of all of the Jewish holidays. More even than the High Holy Days of Rosh Hashanah and Yom Kippur. Secular Jews who, during the year added sizzling bacon to their scrambled eggs and always included pork spare ribs to their Sunday night Chinese food orders were now ridding their houses of any sign or remnants of bread and schlepping up their Passover dishes from the basement. It was a strange and confounding phenomenon and one I could never get my head around. To truly understand Jews and Judaism, one need first understand the existence of kosher-for-Passover toothpaste.

I did not adhere to strict Passover dietary laws. Truth be told, I did not even adhere to lax Passover dietary laws. But I had adopted a Passover tradition of having a nice piece of buttered matza along with a chunk of kashkaval for breakfast. It was a tradition passed on from my grandfather to my father, from my father to me, and one I would gladly pass on to my own children should I ever make it past a second date.

And so I had stopped at Ararat in order to pick up the cheese and who did I run into but Rabbi Jose the Galilean. He was dressed, as was his custom, in black, with a grey beard which nearly ran to the floor.

He lived in the neighbourhood and I would often see him in Ararat where he would like to buy a small piece of halva, the Rabbi had a sweet tooth, drink a cup of Armenian, woe be the person who mistakenly called it Turkish, coffee and chat at the counter about the meaning of life with Mr Zakarian, the shop's jovial and portly owner. It is at the counter where I saw him. He did not, as I said, look very happy.

"Hi Rav," I said, greeting him with the honourific title which he had long earned and deserved "Hag kasher and sameach."

Rabbi Jose the Galilean did not have much reason to be happy. He had married a younger woman who turned out to be a terrible shrew. One who spent all day making fun of him in front of his very own rabbinical students and gave him nothing but tsores. He could not divorce her because she had come with a large dowry he was unable to pay back. His students, finally taking pity on their esteemed rav, raised the money to free him from bondage. The divorce, you would have thought, should have brought Rabbi Jose the Galilean some measure of happiness but alas, it was not to be. His ex-wife had married the town watchman who, as bad luck would have it, became blind and could not watch over anything, much less the town. Jobless, the watchman and his shrew of a new wife, hey I'm just repeating what I heard, had to resort to begging for alms. They finally, reluctantly, because although she might have been a shrew she was not without pride, found themselves in front of Rabbi Jose the Galilean's house. The Rabbi, although having questionable taste in women, was pious and generous, and he ended up taking in his ex-wife and now blind husband. They were now living with him. So he had plenty of reason to be unhappy.

But that wasn't why he did not look happy.

He wasn't happy because of me.

Not wishing me chag sameach in return, he must have been really angry, he said "I heard you have been skipping my section in the Haggadah."

Fucking Lewberg!

That very morning I had told Lewberg that the year prior I had finally convinced my brother and his family to skip over pages 18 and 19. It was a section which was nothing other than commentary by a group of rabbis discussing how many actual plagues the Egyptians had encountered at the Red Sea. It did not, I had argued, add anything to the story, was completely irrelevant and superfluous and, most of all, kept us precious minutes further away from Bubby Judy's pickled brisket. I thought I had made a salient and convincing argument and my family decided, I suspect just to shut me up, to skip over that section with the Rabbis.

The problem was that one of those Rabbis was now standing right in front of me.

"Lewberg?" I asked. I knew it was Lewberg. Who else could it be. The Rabbi liked to bet March Madness and Lewberg would help him lay down his bets.

Rabbi Jose the Galilean shrugged his shoulders and for the briefest of moments the anger dissipated from his body "Those schmucks were giving me Oral Roberts and laying 11.5 points. It was like taking candy from a baby."

"Rav," I said "I'm so sorry. It's just that the seder is so long and that pickled brisket is so good."

"How could you skip my section?" he said. And with that, he stormed out of the store.

At the very same time, my phone vibrated. It was a text from Lewberg.

It said "I think I might have fucked up."

I eat bread on Passover, I do not fast on Yom Kippur, I drive a car and light a fire on shabbat, and I have, more than once, coveted my neighbour's wife. Not my next door neighbour mind you, but a couple who live three blocks down. But you get the drift. I'm not the best of Jews. But of all of the transgressions I have committed, none made me feel worse than the way I threw shade on Rabbi Jose the Galilean.

I called Lewberg and, now being a little angry myself, did not even give him time to apologize.

"Dude," I said "forget about it. What's done is done. Just give me the Rav's address."

"I will text it to you."

Then I said "Oral Roberts?"

"11.5 points," he replied, "I think it is a no brainer."

"Ok, put me down for $100."

Then I went to buy some expensive kosher for passover chocolate and find the rabbi.

Let me say that Rabbi Jose the Galilean's ex-wife was not a shrew. Or, if she was, she was certainly not a shrew to me. She served me very good coffee and macaroons. I'm not so crazy about those macaroons. But still. Then she further ingratiated herself to me by saying. "I read your stories to my husband. They are so amusing."

And her husband, who I had not seen sitting on a rocker in a darkened corner of the room piped up "That Goldfarb is quite a character!"

Then Rabbi Jose the Galilean, a feather duster in his hand, still cleansing his house of the evil hometz, walked into the living room. I leapt to my feet, spilling some of the coffee, and began to launch into my apology. But I was not able to get a word in.

"Aaron Aaron Aaron Aaron," he said, invoking my given Hebrew name which only my father and publisher ever used "I cannot wait for Yom Kippur in order to ask for your forgiveness. I was so small and petty. And to not wish a fellow Jew a kasher pesach- it is a shonda. Please accept my apology."

"Rabbi Rabbi Rabbi," I replied "it is me who should be apologizing to you. I will make sure we recite that section in both Hebrew and English tonight."

"Ach," he said, waving me off with one hand and helping himself to a macaroon with another. "It is a stupid section. I know the Torah and Mishnah backwards and forwards. It is like the air I breathe. I have argued, successfully I might add, with Akiva, Tarfon, and Eliazar. And this is the only thing I am known for. Bah. The number of plagues. It is such a trifle."

"Yes," I said "it is a shame."

"By the way," he added "The number is fifty. Fifty plagues. Don't let anyone tell you different."

"Ok," I said.

"Do you know that Galilean is a term of derision? It is meant to denote a country, how do you say, bumpkin, a fool."

"You are a great sage Rav. After all, it was you who said you could have milk with chicken."

"Ah, so you know that. You surprise me young Aaron."

"Well, I did a little bit of reading. I think you were right."

"What can I tell you. The others were so rigid. So inflexible. But those are matters for another day. We still have to prepare for Pesach. So go Aaron. Go have a chag which is kasher and sameach."

"You too," I said. "By the way, I put $100 on Oral Roberts."

Then Rabbi Jose the Galilean smiled. I think it was the first time I had ever seen him smile.

He said "It's a lock."

Our 7:30 seder did not start until 9:00. We were all hungry and some a little cranky. So my suggestion that we now read pages 18 and 19 was met with a chorus of boos.

"Wait wait wait," I shouted over the tumult. "Here's what I propose. This year we put back the two pages of Rabbi Jose the Galilean but remove the three pages which are commentary from Rabbi Gamliel. It is a net win."

My nieces all flicked through their copies of the Haggadah.

"It's true," said Danna. "Gamliel has more pages. We can skip him and put back Jose the Galilean."

"That's what you want?" Asked my brother, who had long tired of arguing with me.

"I mean," I said, "do we really want the kids to grow up not knowing exactly how many plagues were inflicted on the Egyptians at the Red Sea?"

"You understand how you always get your way?" Said Caroline with a laugh.

"I do. And I appreciate it."

"And what do we get in return?" Asked my brother.

"Well, I did bring you some very good kashkaval," I said. My brother shared in the family tradition.

"Ok," he said. We will blow off Rabbi Gamliel. But it's on you."

That was fine. Rabbi Gamliel lived clear across town and I was unlikely to run into him.

And also, he didn't bet on basketball.

CHATEAU PETRUS

This story was written during the pandemic but takes place many years before. I'm going to go ahead and give away the punchline by telling you it is about me being a germaphobe. I am not a Howie Mandel type of germaphobe or one like Monk, the obsessive-compulsive fictional character played by actor Tony Shalhoub, but I can hold my own. My own particular and peculiar form of germaphobia mostly comes down to my request for full disclosure. If you invite me for dinner, and thank you for thinking of me, just please let me know if one of the kids has a sore throat. Or lice. Don't wait until I have walked in and hung up my coat before asking if I have ever had the chicken pox. That's all I ask. Also, don't tell me it is only a head cold. I don't want a head cold. No matter how good your brisket is. Anyway, that's what this story is about. It takes place at a time before being a germaphobe became the new normal. I was not considered normal. I am still not. I wish I could tell you the telling makes up for the early reveal. I wish I could tell you that you won't see it coming a mile away. I really wish I could. But I am not convinced. You have been warned. Don't come back complaining to me.

My nieces Rena and Danna are at my house looking at old photo albums. They like to amuse themselves by looking at pictures of old girlfriends and then finding out how I screwed up the relationship.

"Who is this?" Asks Rena, holding up a photo.

I take it from her hand and look at it.

"Hillary Shenkman," I say.

"Is that Hillary with one *el* or two *els*?" Asks Danna. I dated two Hillarys. She knows way too much about my past.

"Two *els*," I say.

"She's pretty," says Rena. "Who are these other people?"

"A couple celebrating their 50th wedding anniversary," I reply. "That bottle of wine is very expensive."

"I assume there is a story?" Asks Danna.

"There is," I say.

This story, as these stories tend to be, is about a lie. Really, about two lies. And about two ex-girlfriends.

It was a dinner I did not want to go to. A dinner with Catherine's friends who were absolutely perfectly nice and charming people were it not for the fact they were inveterate wine snobs. But, take wine out of the equation and they were as affable and congenial as a group could be. Now, I still wouldn't have wanted to go to dinner.

But that's on me.

I didn't want to go to the dinner but I liked Catherine and she had cautioned me in the car to 'just try and fit in'. Which I took to mean try not to tell the truth about what you think of wine and wine lovers.

Which was all I was trying to do.

I'm just saying.

But I may have taken it a bit too far. I mean, I really probably shouldn't have brought the picture. But that was later. Anyway, that picture was a reminder of a night which changed my life.

The first lie came as a result of the requisite and predictable question which arose in these gatherings. It was the oenophile's version of when did you lose your virginity. Although, if that were the case, they spent an awful lot of time talking about where and when and with who they lost their virginity. And sometimes, especially after a couple of glasses of wine, they changed their mind about who.

Anyway, I was prepared for the question – 'what was the bottle which did it for you' - because I have watched the movie Sideways about a dozen times.

"Ah, that first bottle," I said, pausing and closing my eyes in feigned reflection like I had seen the others do. Really, I was just thinking about whether it would be ok if I helped myself to a third piece of chicken. "I think I would have to say it was a wine I had in a small vineyard in Montalcino. It was a 2001 Brunello."

As it happened, I had been on a cycling trip in Tuscany with a group of friends and we had stopped and lunched at a small vineyard in Montalcino. Everyone in my group had drunk the Brunello. But not me. I had a coke. One of those mini bottles you can't find any more. It was chilled and delicious. The waiter, if memory serves, was more bemused than aghast and actually poured me a tasting and allowed me to swish it and put my nose to it before filling my glass. He was perhaps, probably most certainly, mocking me, but he did it in such a gentle way that I remember it more than a little fondly.

"The 2001 Brunello was a beast," said Jonathon. Everyone nodded their heads.

Jonathon was Nicole's husband. Nicole was Catherine's best friend. We were in their house. In their dining room. Nicole had made the chicken I was hoping to make myself a bit of a pig with.

"Yes, that 2001 Brunello was a beast," I agreed. "Although, if I have to be completely truthful," I mean, why should I be the only one to lose his virginity once, "there was this Super Tuscan we had the next day in Sienna which was absolutely transcendent."

If you want to play a drinking game. Get together with a group of wine snobs and down a glass every time someone says 'transcendent'.

This triggered a full-fledged and boisterous discussion of wines which had presumably changed lives and futures. I took advantage of the hubbub and distraction to help myself to some more mashed potatoes and the chicken leg I had been coveting. Catherine smiled and winked at me, which could only mean she was drunk or had something in her eye.

I knew I was not being fair. This was really not all that different than a group of my golf buddies discussing their favourite courses. And I knew the conversation was about to turn, as it invariably always did, to a discussion of the best wine they had ever tasted.

The thing is, unlike my golfing pals, I was not entirely convinced this group could tell the difference between Pebble Beach and a mini putt on the Atlantic City boardwalk.

They trotted out the familiar cast of candidates.

"67 Montrachet."

"81 Screaming Eagle."

"59 Domaine Romanee-Conti Tache."

The wines predictably, were all famous, renowned, and expensive. I guess that makes sense. Nobody is going to choose a $12 bottle of 2019 Berringer Cabernet.

When it came to my turn I hesitated and said, "I once had a 49 Chateau Petrus."

"Omg," said Nicole, "a 49 Petrus!!"

I held up my hand "To be fair, it was only a sip."

"I don't think I know this story," said Catherine who was now, all of a sudden looking and sounding much, more sober.

"Well," I said, "you don't really like to hear stories of when I was with other women."

Which was true.

She didn't.

"I think I can make an exception if it involves a 49 Chateau Petrus," she said.

"It was 1999. The Scaramouche Wine Bar," I said, launching into my story "It was the 'go to' place for blind dates. The restaurant was too expensive for dinner so we would go for coffee and a shared dessert. It made a good first impression."

"Btw," interrupted Catherine, "I might mention that Romeo here took to me to Bagel World on our first date."

"You said you liked eggs and onions," I argued.

"Classy," said Jonathon.

"Oh brother. Anyway, I was at Scaramouche on a blind date." I turned to Catherine and said "Ok, it was Hillary Shenkman."

"His Ex," Catherine announced to the table.

I ignored her. "The table next to us was a couple celebrating their 50th wedding anniversary. They ordered the Petrus. The sommelier repeated the year. He said 1949 sir? And the man said yes. The year we got married."

"Oh. That is so sweet," said Nicole's sister Marissa.

"The waiter came with the bottle and decanted it. Then he poured a taste and the man quickly nodded his approval."

I had the room at this point. I had told this story before and knew which points to hit. Which details to highlight. I didn't tell it often because most people did not give a shit about a 1949 Chateau Petrus. But this group did.

"The sommelier filled the glasses and the couple clinked them very gently and toasted each other with a cry of '50 years!' They then both each took a big gulp. 'As good as I remember' said the man."

"You just watched?" Asked Nicole.

"We toasted them with our coffee cups. I think I may have even said mazel tov."

"They were Jewish?"

"No. It was just, you know, in the moment. Then the wife said 'You can't toast with coffee. Let us pour you a glass.' And I said 'Oh that is very kind of you but we couldn't possibly.' I knew the wine was expensive but it turns out I had no clue how much."

Jonathon said "5 gees easy. Maybe 10."

"Right," I said. "There was no way I was going to let him pour me a glass. So I stood firm. And he said, well you should have a sip at least. We waited 50 years between tastings and you two are such a lovely couple you shouldn't have to wait so long."

Catherine said, "Did you really need to add the part of you being a lovely couple?"

"I'm just telling the story. So Hillary now says. I would love a sip. The wife hands Hillary her glass and the man hands me his. We both have a sip and then toast their fifty years."

"And?" Asked Jonathon. "Was it heaven?"

"I don't want to lie," I answer, "I always say it was amazing. But I suspect some of that was because of the price of the wine and my brain telling me what I should think. So the truth is, I don't really remember."

"That's a shame," said Nicole.

"Youth being wasted on the young and all that," I replied. "I have a better memory of the chocolate ganache."

"Wow," said Catherine "That is quite the story. A 1949 Chateau Petrus." I'm not sure she believed me. I don't blame her. She was a wine lover and I had never mentioned the story to her before. And there was a good reason why. Truth is, her bullshit radar is one of the things I liked about her. Which is why I brought the photograph.

"Yup. The waiter even took a photo," I reached into my breast pocket and took out the picture of the four of us surrounding the bottle of wine.

"You carry that with you?" Joked Jonathon.

"Am glad I finally know people who would appreciate the picture," I replied with what was certainly the second lie of the evening.

That story made me the toast of the town. It made me the toast of Catherine. Well, it did for a while anyway. We broke up a few months later. We lived in different worlds and neither of us wanted to keep pretending.

"Good story Uncle Ronnie," says Danna. "Now tell us what really happened."

"Yeah," says Rena, "I call bullshit."

Of course, they are right. There is a little more to the story.

"Ok. The part I don't tell is that two days later I came down with a bad flu and was sick in bed for a week."

The girls look at each other knowingly.

"I knew it would be something like that," says Danna, looking a little too pleased with herself.

"So then why do you hang onto the picture?" asks Rena.

"That picture," I say, "is to remind me to never drink from someone else's glass again."

"That's funny," says Danna. "Are you saying there actually was a time when you shared drinks?"

"Yes," I say.

And then Rena, shaking her head, says "I call bullshit."

BACK FROM THE DEAD

Claire is livid.

I can't say I really can blame her.

You see, the Angel of Death dropped by to return the album he had borrowed - The Band's *Music from Big Pink*. We were about to sit down to dinner so I invited him to join us.

I was now in the kitchen ostensibly to help Claire with the salad, but the salad, in a teak bowl we had bought at Pottery Barn, was already made and sitting, in plain view, on the dining room table. So I was just in the kitchen to get yelled at, albeit in a moderately pitched whisper.

"Why did you invite him?" she hissed.

"It seemed like the polite thing to do. I mean, he could see we were about to eat."

"Who drops by at 6:30?"

"Maybe he is a European Angel of Death," I replied. "They don't eat until 9:00."

"Well what am I going to feed him?"

"Your lasagna and the salad. Plus I got a baguette."

"He eats lasagna?"

"Of course he eats lasagna."

I had no idea if the Angel of Death ate lasagna.

"It's a meat lasagna," she said. "Will that be ok?"

"I don't know, let me ask."

I popped my head out of the kitchen. The Angel of Death had made himself comfortable on the leather couch. Looked like he remembered where I kept the Laphroig.

"Meat lasagna and Caesar salad ok?" I asked. "Claire didn't know we would be having company."

The Angel of Death stood up. "Hey, I really don't mean to impose..."

But I cut him off and directed him to sit back down.

"No, no. It is no imposition. We have plenty. I just wasn't sure if you ate meat."

"Is it lean? I'm trying to watch my weight."

As it happened, it was lean. I had done the grocery shopping myself. I wasn't bringing home any medium chopped ground to Claire. I had learned my lesson. I was about to tell the Angel of

Death but he interrupted me and said "Meat lasagna? What are you, cooking a calf in its mother's milk?"

My heart skipped a beat - he had invoked the ancient Jewish prohibition of mixing milk with meat. I sputtered out a few words in my defence but he cut me off. "I'm just fucking with you dude," he said smiling.

Claire brought out the lasagna and I cut up the baguette. The Angel of Death tucked his napkin into his shirt.

"Don't want to get tomato sauce on my CK shirt," he said. The Angel of Death was a little more dressed up today. Black dress pants and a black silk, I guessed Calvin Klein, shirt. If not for the gold Rolex on his wrist he would have looked a little like a waiter at Cafe Romana.

Claire cut him off a big piece. It barely made a dent in the amount of lasagna in the platter. Claire was a freezer. She always cooked for eight.

The Angel of Death took note of the size of the platter. "That's a lot of lasagna for the three of us," he said. "Are you up for a fourth for dinner?"

I looked at Claire. She gave me a look which said she was not up for a fourth for dinner. It was a look which said she was not up for a third for dinner. Actually, she gave me a look which said, right now, she was not altogether sure she was up for a second for dinner. But I was intrigued. Also, we had a lot of lasagna.

"What did you have in mind?" I asked the Angel of Death as I uncorked a bottle of Barolo I had been saving for a special occasion. I couldn't imagine anything more special than this. Plus, my past experience with the Angel of Death reminded me that things went a lot better if we were both a little drunk.

"Pick any person, living or dead. Sorry, my bad. Not living. I don't have that level clearance. Just dead. And I will arrange for that person to join us for dinner."

So here's the thing. We have all played this game. It is a staple of blind dates and dinner parties. It is such a common game that it has almost become cliché. And here is what happens. Most people will say who they think the other people in the game want to hear, in order to impress, rather than say who they would really like to have dinner with. It's human nature. Then you get a lot of defensive people saying things like "Yeah, well I think Sir Isaac Newton would be fucking interesting." Or, say if people have been drinking "I think it was implied I meant *Carnal Knowledge* Candice Bergen and not *Murphy Brown* Candice Bergen." That kind of thing.

Here's the other thing. If you ever get into a situation where the Angel of Death offers to bring back someone from the dead to join you for dinner, you might want to take a few minutes to think about it. Unless the Angel of Death has said, ok you have ten seconds to decide. But that has not been my experience with the Angel of Death. He has always been pretty chill. Also, and I cannot stress this enough, in fact I should probably have led with it, if you are currently in some sort of relationship, the type of relationship where maintaining the convivial nature of your partner is important, nay essential, then you had better consult with him or her before blurting out a name. Because, as it turned out, lesson learned, once you blurt out a name there are no take backs.

I had played this game before with Claire. More than once. And I knew her answer. It was the answer she gave every time.

"My Nana."

Now when Claire says "My Nana," her by the way 94-year-old grandmother who lived a full life and who had died peacefully in her sleep, everyone else in the room, including me, says "Awwwwww." To reiterate. Including me. Lewberg, on the other hand said, both times, "No, seriously."

But I didn't consult with her. That's on me. That's my bad. If I had even thought about it for three seconds I would have remembered. But I didn't. I just said the first name which came to my head.

Which was -

Italo Svevo.

Wait what?

What the fuck!!!!!

Sorry, nobody in the story said that. I'm just guessing your reaction.

Italo Svevo, nee Aron Ettore Schmitz, was an Italian novelist, playwright, and business man, who was born in the town of Trieste in 1861 when Trieste, which is now a city in Italy, was part of the Austrian Empire. He died in 1928 at the age, I am doing the math in my head, of 67.

It is the 67-year-old Svevo who was now sitting at the dining room table. His close-cropped hair was grey but his bushy moustache was the original black. Unless, of course, there was Grecian Formula in heaven. He had a hat but it was resting on his lap. He looked pretty good for 67. He didn't look like he was going to die that year. So, if any if you are taking notes, it turns out that if the Angel of Death offers to bring someone back from the dead, you get the dead person at the age of their death. Choose wisely my friends.

Svevo was a friend and contemporary of James Joyce and it is that friendship which helped launch his career. His novel, *Zeno's Conscience*, is now considered to be a masterpiece of Italian literature.

His nom de plume was very much Italian but the name given at his circumcision (you see what I did there) was, like mine but with slightly and I think inconsequentially different spelling, Aron. For twenty years, much like my own grandfather Aaron, he worked as a bank clerk while writing and submitting stories.

He was an early practitioner of modernism. He was meta before meta was called meta. That alone would have been enough to draw me to him. But there was a third piece of the puzzle which makes Italo Svevo a compelling and unequalled literary hero. After he got married, Italo, or Aron Ettore as he was then called, earned his living, like me, as a paint salesman.

A paint salesman!

He sold industrial coatings.

Ok, if you look it up it turns out he and his father-in-law were partners in the business.

But c'mon. Let's not quibble. The time is not for hair splitting.

He was a paint salesman!

Which was all well and good and would have been a perfectly reasonable, if a little sentimental, explanation for my rash and unusual choice if not for the fact that, before that very morning, I had never heard of Italo Svevo.

"Are you fucking kidding me now!!!"

That bit is part of the story. That was Claire.

See, Jules had sent me an email that morning with notes on a new story I had written and kindly and generously, finding a tiny bit of similarity in our approach, suggested I look Svevo up. He thought I would really like him. So I did. And then I downloaded his novel on my Kindle, and mentioned to Claire over lunch of tuna and cucumber on a toasted bagel that I had just discovered my new favorite writer. And, "get this" I had crowed, he had been a paint salesman!

Italo Svevo.

So I guess he was on my mind.

Which is why I blurted out his name.

"You knew I wanted my Nana," Claire said very, very softly and then, without even acknowledging Italo, I mean it wasn't his fault I didn't pick her Nana, stormed out of the dining room and into the bedroom.

Italo Svevo was fluent in both Italian and German.

He did not, it turned out, speak English.

I speak English, French, and a little Hebrew.

Fun fact. The Angel of Death only speaks English. Maybe something to know for all those parents enrolling their kids in Introductory Mandarin. He only speaks English. Although when he is drunk, very drunk, he speaks a smattering of Yiddish.

So I didn't get to speak to my new literary hero Italo Svevo. He didn't seem to mind. He was pretty happy to drink my Barolo and then, a few bottles later, my scotch.

I turned on my iPad and showed him the eBook version of his book. He couldn't read it of course but was pleased with the author picture. On closer inspection, we discovered he was now wearing the same hat.

I can't imagine what it would feel like to come back from 1928 and land in a Toronto condo in 2020 but the best word I can find to describe his reaction is nonplussed. I wish I knew how to say that in Italian. It is unlikely anyone would ever blurt out my name in an Angel of Death bring back a person from the dead in order to have dinner game - maybe an ex-girlfriend who wanted to tell me how terrible a boyfriend I was one more time - but it seems unlikely I would be so cool about it.

Claire came out of the bedroom and served us all her famous pecan pie. Italo Svevo said it was "bellissimo." Which made Claire giggle. Although, to be fair, she had drunk a couple of glasses of wine by then.

The Angel of Death suggested we put on some music and Claire got up to choose a record. She played the piano beautifully, had gone to a conservatory for eight years, and had an extensive collection of classical records. I thought she would pick Puccini or Verdi but then I heard the opening bars of BB King's *How Blue Can You Get* from the legendary 1964 *Live at the Regal* recording. It made me remember there was more to like about Claire than her lasagna and pecan pie.

Then the four of us, Claire, the Angel of Death, Italo Svevo and I, sat, ate pie, drank scotch, and listened to BB King.

That's it.

I have no kicker for this story.

No twist ending.

No poignant moment.

Claire's Nana did not show up for tea.

Nobody borrowed any record albums on their way out.

The Angel of Death did not, in a moment of drunken recklessness make James Joyce suddenly appear so he could reacquaint himself with his old friend and offer, since Italian was one of the languages he was fluent in, to translate any questions I might have of Italo Svevo.

And I definitely did not then harangue James Joyce for an hour about run on sentences in Ulysses.

I didn't.

As if.

But c'mon dude, throw in a comma once in a while.

GUINNESS

The summer we turned 12, my friend Stevie Sheen and I decided that a good way to meet girls was to get our names into the Guinness Book of World Records.

The Guinness Book of World Records was an idea cooked up by Sir Hugh Beaver in 1951 when he was the managing director of the venerable Guinness Brewing Company. It appears he was on a shooting expedition in North Slob in County Wexford, Ireland (Definitely the better of the two Slobs) when he came up with the idea. As his shooting party traversed the heaths on horseback, he got into a heated argument (I don't actually know if it was heated but two Irishmen on horses) about which was the fastest game bird in Europe. It was of course the golden plover and shame shame for those amongst you who thought it was the red grouse. Beaver, not patient enough to await the advent of the Internet, thought a book of records was exactly what the world needed at the time. He hired some fact finders and printed one thousand copies, and thus launching one of the most successful and best selling book projects in history.

Just because some guy in Ireland, probably from South Slob, had insisted it had been the red grouse.

By 1972 it had become a huge phenomenon. So much so that our local newspaper, the Montreal Star, carried a regular Saturday article, in a little box tucked into the bottom right corner of the back page of the sports section, which featured the latest record. That Saturday, Stevie and I had read about the first woman who had rowed across the Pacific. Now neither Stevie nor I had access to a rowboat, and I still needed permission to jump off the three meter diving board at our local pool, so a rowing record was likely out of our grasps, but we still thought we could come up with something.

There were, after all, girls out there to be met.

Like Sir Beaver neither Steve and I were too keen to wait another 30 years to go online in order to look up some records, so we made our way to the in real life internet- the Dollard des Ormeaux Public Library. The public library was out near Fairview Shopping Center and Stevie and I had hiked out there, in order to buy french fries and a slushy at Woolworths, quite a few times. I think it was about three miles each way which seems like a long way to walk, along the median of the transatlantic highway mind you (my parents have now both passed away so I can safely reveal this detail), in order to get a slushy but throw in some french fries and it all seems quite reasonable. Stevie was prepared to walk it again but I had an ace up my sleeve- the public library was the one place in the world where my father would drive me, even on a Saturday, his day of rest, with no questions asked. And so, he grabbed a few books he was planning on returning, checked to make sure I had my library card, fortunately did not make some snide comment to

Stevie about whether he was able to read, and we all piled into the Impala and went to the library.

It turned out the library only had one copy of the Guinness Book of World Records.

And that copy was out.

Clearly Stevie and I were not the only boys in Montreal interested in meeting girls.

It was due back in two weeks.

Two weeks later I returned to the library with my father minus Stevie, who had decided that perhaps there was an easier way of meeting girls than eating one hundred hot dogs in twenty minutes.Also, that one trip to the library in a year was enough.

I took the book out. It was the 1968 edition. I read it through twice. Kept it three weeks longer than I should have. Paid a $1.75 cent fine. Incurred a pretty serious lecture from my father about being responsible. And didn't find a single record that I could remotely come close to breaking.

So I forgot about getting my name into the Guinness Book of World Records.

Until 50 years later.

In the summer of 2021 three friends and I took a bucket list trip to play golf in Ireland. Our friend Jeff, who had gone the year before, had told us that the tour of the Guinness brewery was really worthwhile. I told him the only way I would end up on that tour was if it rained for five days straight.

I went on the fourth day.

Playing golf in the Irish wind and sideways rain on a links course is actually a really fun thing to do. It creates a strong sense of comraderie and a lifetime of stories.

To repeat. A really fun thing to do.

Once.

A little less fun twice.

Pretty miserable three times.

My golf partners had gone up to Portmarnock to play that famed course in the driving rain. Fourth time, they reckoned, would be the lucky charm.

I stayed in Dublin and went to the Guinness Brewery.

Now I'd like to tell you the tour of the Guinness Brewery was really interesting but I only lasted ten minutes. Barely made it out of the lobby. The combination of fermenting malt and yeast yielded a most unpleasant odor which made me gag. It almost made me want to quit drinking beer. I said almost. So instead, I snuck out and went across the street to a pub and ordered the beer I would have gotten for free had I lasted another forty-five minutes until the end of the tour.

The pub was nearly deserted which made sense because although Dubliners take their reputation as prodigious drinkers quite seriously, it was not yet 11:00 AM and most were no doubt still trying to digest the gallon of oil and lard which had accompanied their traditional fry up breakfast. The bartender, a cherubic red head with a matching mariner beard was polishing mugs and gave me the once over before addressing me.

"American?" He asked.

"Canadian," I answered.

"Tourist?"

"Golf trip."

"Aye. Shame it's lashing down. You just need the right gear."

What I needed was an ark. But I didn't say that.

"Are you Scottish?" I asked. The 'aye' was a dead giveaway.

"Scottish! Feck off!!"

"But you said aye," I protested.

"I'm from Derry. Northern Ireland. We say aye."

"Ah right," I said "Londonderry." I knew my geography.

"Are you after gettin a beating? It's Derry."

"I'm sorry. I'm from Canada."

"I'm just taking the piss. You've been over at Guinness have you?"

"Yes."

"A big destination for the tourists so it is," he said.

"It was very interesting," I said "I took the tour." I didn't mention the gagging

"I hear they give you a right nice pour at the end of the tour."

"Yes," I said. The brochure did mention a tasting.

"You must have quite the thirst on you." He said handing me a pint of foamless Guinness.

"Aye," I said, hoping he wouldn't think I was making fun.

"That Guinness World Record book is named after the brewery. Not a lot of people know that."

"That's very interesting," I said, not wanting to say that it was actually called the Guinness Book of World Records. "When I was young, I thought that having my name in the book would help me meet girls," I said.

"How did that turn out for you?" He asked.

"Not so good." I said with a laugh.

"Ach. Most of those records are shite. A bakery up in Galway holds the record for most cookies baked in a day. Total shite."

"Yes," I agreed, remembering the book I had borrowed from the library. "The majority of the records are pretty silly." I hadn't worked up the nerve to say shite yet. "I once tried to break the record for fastest time to peel and eat ten oranges. I didn't make it past three."

"Jaysus," he said "that's shite."

"Yeah," I agreed. "Total shite."

"Of course there are some good ones," he said.

"Yeah?"

"Yeah. Oldest man to break the four minute mile."

"Really?" I asked "how old?"

"41. And he was an Irishman so he was."

"Who?"

"Yer man Eamon Coghlan."

"That's pretty good," I said "Fair play to him." Ok, so now I had worked up a quite a lot of nerve.

"If you don't mind me asking. How old a man are you?"

"62."

"Well, there you go then."

"What do you mean?"

"That's 21 years older than Eamon. That's fecking good that is."

"I don't really run. I'm not sure I could even drive a mile in four minutes."

"Who said anything about running," he said with a smile. "You just have to say you are after going for the record. That's mighty impressive that is. You'll have the ladies coming for miles."

"Nobody's going to believe that," I said.

"Aye. You might be right." Again he gave me the once over " You don't look like much of an athlete."

As we were talking, a man had settled into the stool next to me and ordered a double whiskey.

"I apologize for listening in on your conversation like," he said in a conspiratorial whisper, "but are you really after getting your name in the book?"

"A lifelong dream," I said. It wasn't really. It was a dream interrupted by fifty years of life.

"Well the wife is going over to Galway with her choir group. She's meeting up with other choir groups from all over Ireland. They're after setting a world record. A Guinness record like."

"In singing?"

"Not exactly."

"Not exactly?"

"No."

The next day the sun came out. Not a breath of wind. My crew drove up towards Belfast to play at North County Down- one of the most storied golf courses in all of the world.

To their amazement, befuddlement and, dare I say, disgust, I did not go with them. Instead, on that most glorious of Irish days, I rented a car and drove west to Galway and took part in a Guinness World Record.

There were 2700 of us.

All dressed as leprechauns.

You can look it up. Most people ever assembled in one place dressed as leprechauns. Galway. July 20, 2021.

I have a picture.

Largest Gathering of People Dressed Like Leprechauns

See?

That's me over there.

In the green.

THE REMINDER

Photograph © Laura Chouette / Unsplash

The first time Goldfarb had sex with his new girlfriend, right in the middle, although to be fair, it felt like the middle for him but could have been anywhere for her, right in the middle she screamed out "Oh my god, Mrs. Flackowitz!" The line was a little unconventional and not one which he was familiar with but he chose to focus more on the 'Oh my god' and less on the 'Mrs. Flackowitz'.

He wasn't going to lie.

He was pretty pleased with himself.

What with it being the first time and all.

So, he began to retrace the sequence of events which had led to this moment in the hope he would be able to recreate it, but did not get very far when his girlfriend explained it was not a cry of Judeo/Yiddish exaltation but rather the name of her grade 3 homeroom teacher.

Which she had suddenly just remembered.

That struck him as a peculiar thing to remember while having sex, whether in the beginning, middle or end, but being a firm believer in the 'even bad pizza is still good pizza' adage, and having been on a bit of a pizza drought lately, he decided to take it both in stride and good humor.

The second time Goldfarb had sex with his new girlfriend, early on, if it had been a book it would have been chapter 5 or 6, she suddenly cried out "Nutmeg!" Which might very well have been some sort of adoring nickname, but after the Mrs. Flackowitz episode Goldfarb knew better.

"Nutmeg," he repeated.

And she said "Yes. I just remembered I need it for my muffin recipe."

This time Goldfarb decided to confront her. "Do you think you should be thinking about your muffin recipe in the middle of our, of our, you know, lovemaking?"

"I wasn't thinking about it silly. I just remembered it."

The third time Goldfarb had sex with his new girlfriend he got another "Oh my god." They had only just started. They were somewhere between the dedication and the table of contents. And then, yet another "Oh my god!" Which ordinarily would have been cause for celebration but, you know, fool him thrice.

So he waited for it.

She had just remembered that today was her Uncle Nate's birthday.

"I better call him," she said.

"Now?" Asked Goldfarb.

"Yes, before I forget."

Lewberg thought Goldfarb was crazy for thinking of breaking up with his new girlfriend.

"This woman actually agrees to have sex with you," he said one night while they were having drinks at the Firkin. "So it jogs her memory a bit. Big deal. You should take it as a compliment."

"Look," Goldfarb replied. "I'm not saying it is the end of the world. I'm just saying it is a thing. Will you agree that it is a thing?"

Lewberg drained his Kettle and cranberry and signaled the waitress for another.

"Yes councilor," he said. "I will concede that it is a thing. But not a thing worth breaking up for."

"Lewberg," Goldfarb replied, ordering a second drink of his own. "Not only does she not think it is a thing but she thinks me thinking it is a thing is actually the thing. It is a world gone mad. I have to break up with her."

Solly was no more sympathetic, but at least he was a little more curious.

"Let me ask you this," he said. "Once she remembers something, does it end the festivities?"

"It doesn't end the festivities," Goldfarb replied, "but it puts into question what the hell we were celebrating in the first place."

Solly shook his head and said "I can't help you man. This is on you."

Goldfarb said "I am definitely going to break up with her."

Amanda at least, was sympathetic. Although, truth be told, she was never a big fan of Goldfarb's new girlfriend. "You are making the right decision Harold," she said. "You can do much better."

"I'm not crazy right? I mean it's not normal."

"It isn't Harold. It's not normal at all. You have to break up with her."

"I am," said Goldfarb. "I am going to break up with her."

Just then Goldfarb received a text from his new girlfriend. He looked up at Amanda. Then back at his phone.

"Hey Amanda thanks for the chat. But I have to go."

"Is everything alright?" Asked Amanda.

"Yes," replied Goldfarb. "I just have to go help out a friend. She can't remember where she left her sunglasses."

STOCKING THE POND

I get up at 3am to go to the bathroom. When I get back to bed I see I have a text from Lewberg.

"Do you still have that bucket of coins?" No 'hello'. No 'how are you'.

I text him back "What are you doing up?"

"Australian Open. I have a five-player parlay."

That makes sense. Lewberg likes to gamble. Mostly sports betting but he really likes to bet on everything. He can't watch a game without having a few dollars on it.

"Five player parlay?"

"I need Putinseva to win the third set."

"Putinseva?"

"Yulia Putinseva. From Kazakhstan." Lewberg sounds annoyed I don't know an obscure tennis player who has made it to the second round.

"OK," I say.

"You still have that bucket?"

I am pretty sure nobody else in the world is having this conversation. But this is par for the course with Lewberg.

"Lewberg. If you are strapped for cash I will write you a cheque. We don't have to revert to the bucket of coins. Those days are long gone."

The bucket of coins had started, as you would imagine, as a jar of coins. Coins emptied from my pant and coat pockets at the end of an evening. They would first land on the dresser or night table, and then eventually wind up in the jar. Pennies, nickels, dimes and quarters. The one jar turned into two and then I think my cleaning lady, correctly assessing that I was not hosting elaborate dinner parties, transferred the contents of the two jars into a glass serving bowl. Their residency in the glass bowl however was short lived as the coins were soon overflowing, and so they unceremoniously made their way to another receptacle I had no use or would ever have any use for - a paint bucket. I still have it, it is nestled in the corner of my bedroom.

"Yes" I reply. "I still have it."

"Then why do you live in that junkie house?" Lewberg texts with a smiling emoji.

Three AM and Lewberg is making jokes. It is, in part, a testament to the folklore about the bucket and how its existence has become ingrained in my life and in my story.

In this instance, he is referring to the time I had invited my friend Eric, his wife Randy, and his twin boys over for a backyard BBQ in an attempt to reciprocate for the many meals I had had at their house. I rented a small bungalow, it was the only house on the street which had not yet been torn down and replaced with a modern behemoth. The house was admittedly ramshackle and I had not done much in the way of renovations or decorations. This led one of the boys to innocently and famously ask why I lived in "such a junkie house." His parents, aghast at their son's words, immediately demanded he apologize for the slight. He, confused by his parents' consternation, mounted a defense "But," he argued, "I know he is rich. I saw his bucket of coins in the house."

The irony, of course, is that at the time, that bucket of coins, was pretty much all of the money I had in the world. I had transitioned careers - my Uncle Henri had fired me for the third and last time - and had gone into hock and credit card debt in order to launch an eBook business at a time when eBooks did not exist. For a time, that bucket funded every pizza slice, every cup of coffee, every newspaper which passed through my front door portal. I never counted it. Never wanted to know how much was in there for fear it would depress me too much. It couldn't have been more than a couple of hundred bucks. But the kid thought he had stumbled onto El-Dorado.

Luckily, my fortunes turned but I continued to tell the story. Along with the time my electricity got turned off and the unlikely friendship I had forged with the lady from the American Express credit department. I joke about it but they were tough times. I had to borrow money from both my father and my brother. I have since moved to another, only slightly less junkie house, but I still have the bucket of coins. Somehow, I just haven't been able to part with them.

"Can I borrow them?" Lewberg asks.

I, of course, know better than to ask Lewberg why. Nothing good can come of it. I will get embroiled in some sort of scheme which skirts both the law and morality and will have nobody to blame but myself.

So instead I say "My pleasure," knowing it is very likely I will never see them again. In a way, Lewberg is doing me a favor. He is helping me make a decision I have been unable to make myself.

"You don't want to know why?" He asks.

I don't answer right away. I am trying to formulate a witty comeback but take a bit too long. Lewberg interprets my silence as tacit acquiescence.

"It's for my Uncle Nate," he volunteers. "He didn't make it down to Florida this winter and he is going crazy. He used to spend every morning with his metal detector, the Bounty Hunter 1000, scouring the beach for lost treasure. So he's taken to tracking down every coin in his apartment to see if he can find something old and valuable. He even has a magnifying glass to look at dates and imperfections. He bought books and spends hours on the internet researching."

"Jesus," I say, "poor Nate. So where do I come in?"

"He is out of coins. My cousin Shelly said he could really use a new batch. She said nothing would thrill him more than getting a bucket of coins."

"Ah. Got it. So you told her…"

Lewberg cuts me off.

"So I told her I think I knew a guy."

Lewberg's Uncle Nate is a curmudgeon's curmudgeon. Think Walter Matthau in *The Sunshine Boys*. I saw him a lot more later in life when he retired to Florida. We sometimes golfed with him or had lunch at the deli. He sent a lot of things back. He was a misery, almost a caricature. I would like to say he got worse after he lost his wife, Lewberg's aunt, to cancer but he was always a little glum. A little stoic. Even back in the day.

Somehow, we developed a tradition where he would take us, Lewberg, Goldfarb, and I, fishing once a summer. It was always the third Saturday in July. It was, we discovered one year, rain or shine and no rain checks would be issued. He would provide the fishing rods, the bait, a six pack of beer which we could divide however we decided, and a dozen chocolate donuts from Tim Horton's. We would fish for three hours. From 8am to 11 am.

Now there is nothing unusual about early morning fishing. Nate had a cottage up near Bracebridge in Ontario's Muskoka region. In theory, we should have driven up on Friday night, slept over, then gone fishing the next morning. But Nate didn't want us sleeping over. Instead, we drove for two hours early on Saturday morning.

The cottage was on a tiny, pristine lake called, I can't make this stuff up, Pickerel Lake. Pickerel, for you city folk, is a type of fish. The type of fish which was found in the lake. Now you would think this is the lake where Uncle Nate, Lewberg, Goldfarb and I would have gone fishing.

But you would be wrong.

Instead, we loaded up Uncle Nate's truck and drove about twenty minutes south on Highway 11, just before the Gravenhurst cut off, where we turned east at exit 42. Exit 42 by the way is the exit we drove by on the way to Nate's cottage.

"Why can't we just meet him there?" Goldfarb and I must have argued the first year. And Lewberg must have said "because he doesn't trust you." Which was fair enough and we never questioned it again.

Now if you drive eighteen minutes east after getting off on exit 42 you are going to reach a place called Miller's Trout Farm. This is where Mr. Miller and the Miller kinfolk stock a moderately sized pond with trout. They basically filled the pond up with so much trout that it was impossible not to catch something. I think it might have been $25 per car and then $10 for three hours on a row boat. The Miller motto was "catch and release but one" - each person on the boat could bring home one trout. By the end of the day Uncle Nate would have four trout in the cooler which had originally held the beer. We would release the early caught trout because nobody wanted to drink out of cans which had lain with the fish. I don't know what Uncle Nate did with those fish. I assumed he ate them. It's not like we ever had a cookout or anything. We fished for three hours. Then his duty was done. It was if it had been court mandated.

I don't know how many summers we did that. It could have been ten.

And for ten years, every time Uncle Nate would make the sharp left turn at the faded and splintered wood sign which said, in yellow paint, Miller's Trout Farm, he would exclaim "If you want to get laid, you go to a whorehouse."

Every time.

I don't remember him saying much of anything else. It's not like he was taking us to a whorehouse. He was taking us fishing. He never elaborated. Never told us his philosophy on life. We got it. A stocked trout farm. Still, it got to be a thing. The anticipation of him saying the line.

"If you want to get laid, you go to a whorehouse."

Plus, the beer, the donuts, and catching fish we knew we were going to catch.

Which is why, after Lewberg's text, I know what I am going to do.

I am going to stock the bucket with my own trout.

I am going to seed it with some rare coins.

Now I have some coins I had collected. Some ancient Greek and Roman coins. Some silver dollars. But those won't do. They would be too obvious. So I call my coin guy. Lewberg is not the only person with a guy.

Nothing fancy - three pennies, three nickels, three dimes. Late 1800's, turn of the century, early 1900's. The nine have a face value of 48 cents and a collector's value of about $300. Won't make me even for the years of fishing, but it will get me close.

The coins come by courier and, like a lotto hostess shuffling ping pong balls, I mix and intermingle them into the contents of my bucket of coins. As I plunge my hands deep into the bucket, grabbing and redistributing fistfuls of coins, I am reminded of the time my friend Karen brought her kids over for Halloween and I, no big surprise, was completely unprepared with any treats so instead dragged out my bucket of coins and offered a two-fisted free for all instead. The kids, wide-eyed and excited, each took turns and, if I remember correctly, the option for one re-do in order to extract the biggest bounty. I had candy the next year and the year after that but the kids insisted instead on the bucket of coins. By then they had cagily figured out how to aim for the parts with the most silver I think we ended up doing that for about five years. Then the kids got older and trick or treating, even with the prospect of free money, became less appealing. And also, a little less rewarding. Finally, one year, her youngest, Joshua, left me with a parting "lots of pennies dude" jibe which more or less put an end to that tradition.

Lewberg arrives a few minutes later and I ceremoniously present him with the bucket.

"Regards to Uncle Nate," I say.

"I really appreciate it," says Lewberg. "He is really down in the dumps. Starting to be nice to people."

"Well it is my pleasure. He is welcome to anything he finds."

"Is he going to find anything?"

I know Lewberg can keep a secret but I also know he might get a kick out of knowing I got screwed out of $300 worth of valuable coins. It is a win-win. So I just say "A lifetime of loads for a coin laundry." But when Lewberg gets to the door, I can't help myself. "I might have sprinkled in a handful of valuable coins," I say smiling. "If you want to get laid...."

"No shit?"

"What can I say? We curmudgeons have to stick together."

"You're a good man," says Lewberg.

A week goes by. I text Lewberg. "Any word from Nate."

"Yeah," replies Lewberg, "and I quote. 'You brought me a bucket of shit.'"

I try again a week later.

"Any word?"

Lewberg texts back "Bucket of shit."

Week three, Uncle Nate finds the first of the planted coins. Then another on week four.

"Some of this isn't complete shit," is the report I get from Lewberg. I guess it feels pretty good. I am bringing a little cheer during difficult times. It is worth every cent.

Then, on week nine, a text from Lewberg:

"Did you plant a 1969 Canadian dime?"

I text back "No."

"Are you sure?"

I am sure. A 1969 dime would be worth ten cents. It isn't one of my trout.

"I'm sure."

Lewberg texts me an image. It is of a 1969 Canadian dime. I have never seen it before.

"It's not my plant. Why are you wasting my time with this?"

"It has a large print date. Very rare."

"Fuck off!"

"Nate just got it appraised. It's worth $25,000."

"Jesus!" I say. "It was in my bucket?"

"Yup. Nate is going through the contents with a fine-tooth comb. Said the large date just jumped out at him."

"Twenty-five grand?"

"Maybe more if it is in mint condition."

"I could have paid my electricity bill."

"Worse. You could have used it to buy a slice of peperoni."

"True."

"He's going to donate it to Sunnybrook Hospital. In honor of my late aunt. He wanted to know if you were ok with that."

"Yeah," I say, "that's a fantastic idea. Catch and release eh?"

"Yeah," says Lewberg. "Catch and release."

"Wow. Twenty-five grand.

"Yeah."

"He went through every coin in the bucket?"

"Yeah."

"I guess I didn't have to stock the pond after all."

"Yeah, well us Lewbergs don't need any help to get laid."

SHPRINTZA

I met Siobhán Rooney on an Air Canada flight from Toronto to Tel Aviv in the summer of 1980. I was 21, had recently graduated with a useless degree in political science, and had absolutely no idea what I wanted to do with my life. I figured a trip to Israel would be something I could do in the meantime. Siobhán, in a sense, was in the same boat. She had also just graduated, from Tufts in her hometown of Boston. Flying from Toronto proved to be cheaper than New York.

We spoke for about an hour before exchanging names. She had a pretty thick Boston accent. The 'Southie' brogue which Matt Damon and Ben Affleck later showcased in Good Will Hunting. Am a little embarrassed to say I tried to show off.

"Ah Siobhán," I said, "the name which does not sound like it is spelled."

"My cross to bear," she said with a smile. "And it's not even my first name. It is my middle name. My given name is even more difficult."

"Wow, your parents really went to town."

"You have no idea."

"Ok, go ahead and hit me. I can't wait to hear it."

"I could tell you but then I would have to kill you," she laughed.

"Fair enough. I can wait."

But I didn't have to wait long. Two minutes later the stewardess was in our aisle with our in-flight meals. What she then said gave birth to this story.

"I have a kosher meal for a Shprintza Rooney."

"That's me," said Siobhán.

I looked at her. I guess gaped at her would be a better description.

"Irish Catholic," she said with a shrug. "But I heard the kosher meals were better. For once I can take advantage of my given name."

"Shprintza? Your given name is Shprintza."

"Yup."

"Go on," I said.

"It's a long story," she said.

"Well," I said, peeling back the cover of my non-kosher roast chicken which did not look nearly as good as her schnitzel, "I'm not going anywhere."

This is the story she told me.

Boston, 1960

"Over my dead body," Miriam declared, as she ladled the chicken soup into a bowl.

"A thousand dollars is a lot of money," replied Reuben. "We could use the money."

"Have you lost your mind, Reuben? Shprintza?!?! We are going to call our first born Shprintza?"

"It's just a name. A name doesn't define who you are or who you will be. Can I have another matzo ball?"

"I don't want to hear another word about it. Throw that newspaper out. What kind of crazy person takes an ad out like that? Mary Elizabeth dear," she said, addressing the also-pregnant woman who was scrubbing a pot. "Just soak it overnight. It will be much easier to clean in the morning."

Miriam's mother-in-law paid for the cleaning lady. A favor she never forgot to remind her of.

"Yes, ma'am," Mary Elizabeth said, only too happy to stop scrubbing and get off her feet.

"Just take the trash out and head on home. Your feet must be killing you. Reuben! Reuben! Give Mary Elizabeth the newspaper to throw into the trash."

Mary Elizabeth took the trash and grabbed the newspaper. The trash she threw into the big grey garbage bin. But the newspaper, the Jewish Advocate, the newspaper she put into her purse.

"Read it again," Billy said, as he turned down Gunsmoke.

Mary Elizabeth put on her reading glasses and opened the newspaper to the notice on the second to last page which she'd circled and highlighted in yellow. *"I will pay a $1000 honorarium if you name your first-born daughter after my late grandmother Shprintza Nachama Goldberg of blessed memory who perished in Auschwitz. Only serious applicants need apply.* There's a Boston phone number."

"Crazy lady," snorted Billy.

"A thousand dollars is a lot of money," Mary Elizabeth said.

"Darling, no Jewish woman is going to give a Catholic $1000 to name her baby Shpinger."

"Shprintza. I looked it up. It means hope."

"Mary Elizabeth Rooney. You don't think it's hard enough growing up poor in south Boston, and now you want to saddle your daughter with some crazy name of some dead old lady?"

"It means hope. I kinda like it. We would be honoring her memory. Maybe bring us and her some good luck."

"That first Shprintza," he said, "sounds like she had no good luck at all."

"$1000. That's free money. She is already bringing us good luck. I am going to call in the morning."

"Mary Elizabeth. If that crazy Jewish lady hands you $1000 to give your daughter the name of her dead grandmother then you can go ahead and call me Moses because our house is nothing but a house of miracles. Now come over here and I'll rub your feet."

"I'm Janice. On the phone you said your name was Mary Elizabeth Rooney. Is it Mary Elizabeth or just Mary?"

"I wish it were just Mary. But it has been Mary Elizabeth all my life. It is my cross to bear for being Irish."

"I get it," Janice said with a smile.

"Irish Catholic ma'am. Janice. On both sides. On all sides. I didn't know if that would be a problem."

"It's not," said Janice, "we are all god's children. And being a redhead is a bonus."

"Well it's about time that worked to my advantage."

"Well come on in. Where did you hear about my situation?"

"In the Jewish advocate. I work for a Jewish family. I can even make a challah." Mary Elizabeth did not know why she had said that. She was a little bit nervous.

"Well I would love to try it. Maybe you can even give me a baking lesson. Can I make you a coffee?"

"Yes please. Cream and sugar please."

"When are you due?"

"Four weeks. But if the good Lord said today, he wouldn't get any argument from me. You never had kids?"

"I wasn't able to. Probably a good thing. My husband would have left me if I had called our daughter Shprintza. Although he did leave me. But for completely different reasons."

"I'm sorry, ma'am."

"Don't be, Mary Elizabeth. Tell me, what were you thinking of calling your daughter before this?"

"Well Billy, he's my husband. Billy is partial to Dorothy. It was his mother's name. We would call her Dot."

"Dot Rooney. That's nice. A whole lot nicer than Shprintza Rooney," she said smiling. "I mean, I understand why everyone is saying no. It's quite a mouthful. But $1000 is all I can afford."

"Well at least Shprintza is only one name. I have been Mary Elizabeth my whole life."

"You might be right," replied Janice Goldberg. "Here, let me show you a picture," she said as she handed Mary Elizabeth a creased 3 by 5 black and white photo.

It was a family portrait. It looked like it may have been taken by an actual photographer.

"Here," Janice pointed to a pigtailed ragamuffin kneeling in the front. "That was Shprintza. They said she was a real troublemaker."

"What's that next to her feet?" asked Mary Elizabeth.

Janice chuckled. "That's her pet chicken Haman. My Uncle Rachum said that chicken followed her everywhere."

"You see the boy standing tall in the back? That's Rachum. My uncle. He and my mother are the only ones in the picture who survived the camps. Everyone else perished."

"My lord," said Mary Elizabeth.

Just then the phone trilled.

"Will you excuse me?"

"Yes, of course." Mary Elizabeth examined the photo. It was too horrible to even imagine.

When Janice Goldberg came back, she had a pained expression on her face.

"I am so sorry, Mary Elizabeth."

"That call was from a family in Boro Park. You know, in Brooklyn?"

Mary Elizabeth did not know Boro Park.

"Anyway, they are very orthodox. And very poor. They were thrilled to get the $1000. And although it isn't their firstborn daughter - it will be their ninth kid - they are very comfortable with the name. It isn't even that uncommon in the orthodox community. So, my grandmother's memory will be honored. I am so sorry."

Nine kids. Oh my Lord. "Thanks for letting me know, Miss Goldberg... Janice. I am real happy for you."

Janice Goldberg pressed a $100 bill onto Mary Elizabeth's hand. "Here, Mary Elizabeth. Please take this."

"Oh no, Mrs. Goldberg. I'll be alright."

"For the baby. For Dot. You can buy her a nice crib. Please. It will make me feel better."

"Okay, Janice. Thank you kindly. I will buy a crib. For Dot. Much appreciated."

Then Mary Elizabeth got her coat, closed the door, and took the bus back home.

"$100?" said Billy.

"She just went and gave you $100?"

"Yes, she was nice. She told me all about her grandmother. Well, the little she knew. She was from a small little village in Poland. Was very poor. Barely had enough food to eat."

And then she whispered, not loud enough for Billy to hear, "And she also had a pet chicken."

"Sounds like us," said Billy with a laugh. "We are from a small village in Boston. C'mon now. Let's watch some TV."

Mary Elizabeth loved to take Dot out for long walks. She proudly pushed her stroller through the streets of Boston every day. Dot was a beautiful baby and a day rarely went by without a flurry of oohs and ahs from fellow Bostonian denizens. Sometimes she liked to get on the bus with her stroller and baby and go for walks in the leafy gentrified neighborhoods many blocks from her home.

So it was just by chance, one unseasonably warm April afternoon, that she found herself right in front of Janice Goldberg's townhouse just as she was walking out the door.

"Mary Elizabeth Rooney! I can't believe it! And oh my goodness, is this Dot? She's an angel."

"Yes, Mrs. Goldberg. Dorothy Molly Rooney. But we call her Dot. She is my bundle of joy."

"Now Mary Elizabeth. You call me Janice. Can I hold her?"

"Of course you can, Janice. And we just love the crib. Don't we, Dot?"

Janice Goldberg held the baby in her arms. "Well this just makes my day."

Mary Elizabeth proudly watched Janice Goldberg coo over her baby. She could tell she was a good woman. "Janice?" She asked. "How are things over in Brooklyn? In... Boro Park. How is baby Shprintza?"

Janice handed Dot back to Mary Elizabeth.

"Well you'll never believe it," she said with a smile. "It was a boy. The doctors were sure she was having a girl, but boy oh boy did they get it wrong. So Shprintza is now Shmuel. They sent me a picture. A beautiful boy. But not as beautiful as Dot."

"Oh, Janice, I'm so sorry."

"Oh, don't be. Can never be sorry about a healthy baby. Two healthy babies. They wanted to give me back the money, but I insisted they keep it. I think my grandmother, may she rest in peace, would have understood."

"Am sure she would," said Mary Elizabeth.

"Will you come in for a coffee or maybe something stronger?" Said Janice.

"Another time," said Mary Elizabeth. "But I can't have anything stronger," she smiled and rubbed her belly, "because I am pregnant."

"So let me get this straight," I said. "You get Shprintza Siobhán and your sister gets Dot?"

"Yup, classic middle child syndrome," she says.

"There is another?"

"Another girl. Elizabeth Mary."

"But that's..."

"The reverse of my mother's name."

"Wow. They really did a number on you."

"It's not so bad. Shprintza is only my legal name. On my passport and birth certificate. Even my driver's license says Siobhán. Sometimes I forget it altogether."

"Unless you need it for kosher food."

"Right."

"Btw. How was the schnitzel?"

"It was delish."

"So Israel?"

"I'm going to work on a kibbutz. Do a little sightseeing."

"So no conversion?" I asked with a smile.

"Nope. I am Irish Catholic through and through. I sang in our church choir."

"Shprintza though, seriously? It is honestly kinda hard to believe. Your father must have been very supportive."

"You need to understand the Irish and our superstitions. Everything is a sign. My pa couldn't compete against a sign."

"I thought it was good luck to be named after a Saint."

And then Shprintza Siobhán Rooney, in her thick southie accent said, "Nah, that is a bubbe meise."

RASHI'S DIME

I don't know what it is with these fucking shoelaces. I am on my way home from my daily walk in the ravine and it is the third time I have to stop, take off my gloves, and tie them up again. I refuse to do a double knot because A. I am not an 8-year-old boy, and B. Because I know I will never untie the double knot and I will become the guy who slips in and out of his running shoes, or even uses a shoehorn, because he is too lazy to untie the knot. Anyway, I step off the walking path in order to let the couple walking their dog behind me get past, and bend over to retie my right shoe.

And that is when I see it.

A dime.

On the ground.

Heads up.

You almost never see a dime on the ground. A lot of pennies. Some quarters. Sometimes even the odd Loonie. But you almost never see a dime.

I don't know why that is.

My friend Becky says finding a dime is supposed to be a sign or message from someone you know who has passed away. But I don't know. Seems a little subtle. I mean, a rainbow I could understand. A dime on the ground is a little like a whisper at a rock concert. Anyways, this is not the time to be picking up strange things from the ground. I mean, I have a mini bottle of Purell in my pocket. What am I going to do? Pick up the dime, put it in my coat pocket, then take out the Purell and sanitize my hands, then wash my hands again when I get home? Then what? Keep the dime in my coat pocket?

No. I don't need that aggravation. If someone wants to send me a message from beyond, let them use WhatsApp like the rest of us.

So I go home and don't think about it again until the next day when I go on my walk. This time, my shoelaces are fine. I have, in fact, switched shoes. But I stop to take a drink from my water bottle very near the spot where I tied my shoes for the third time yesterday.

The dime is still there.

Which makes perfect sense. This isn't a golf course where every second group is going into the trees looking for lost golf balls. This is a patch of grass a few yards away from a foot path. There is no reason why anyone would find it.

I drink my water and go on my way.

The next day I don't even make a pretense. I make a beeline for the dime.

It is still there.

I leave it undisturbed.

When I get home, I call Becky.

"I found a dime on my way home from the ravine," I say. I don't say I have seen it three days in a row.

"Someone is trying to send you a message," she replies without missing a beat. Then she says "I wonder who it is?"

"I have no idea," I say.

Then she says "Where are you keeping it?" I don't tell her I didn't actually pick it up. Instead, I say "In my jar with all the other messages from dead people."

"No really," she says.

"No really what?" I reply.

"Where did you put it?"

"What difference does it make. It's a weird question."

Then she says "I don't think you picked it up."

I don't talk for a second. Then I say. "How do you know?"

And she says "I've never seen you pick up anything in your life. There is no way you picked up a dime."

"You're right," I admit. "I didn't pick it up."

"You have to go back and pick it up. Someone is sending you a message."

"Becky, you know I don't believe in this nonsense. I was just telling you in passing."

"Go back tomorrow and pick it up. If it is still there, it is a sign."

"Nobody is sending me a message."

And she says "I don't know." But she says it in that way where the word 'know' takes about ten seconds to pronounce. It is very annoying.

I say "Goodbye crazy person." And then I hang up.

But now I am beginning to think maybe I should have picked up the dime. If someone is trying to send me a message, who am I to be blocking the calls.

I get up early the next morning and drive to the spot near the walking path. I park illegally across the street and go to the spot.

Needless to say, the dime is not there. I search for about twenty minutes. Some passerby with a video camera would have gotten some pretty good footage of an old Jew on his hands and knees looking for a dime.

Damn.

Somebody else got my message.

I find a bench and call Becky. I wake her up.

"It's not there," I say.

"What's not there?" She asks.

"The dime. The dime is not there."

"What dime? What time is it?"

"Becky, my dime. My message dime. It's not there."

And then she says "Ok."

I say "Ok?"

"Look, if it's not there it's not there. There will be other dimes."

"What the fuck. Yesterday you were telling me it is a sign and today you are saying there will be other dimes? What kind of friend are you?" Now I was upset.

"Calm down. I am not the keeper of the dimes. It's just a Bubbe Meise. It's not a big deal. Besides, if you saw it the next day then maybe it would have been a sign. But it was gone. It was probably a wrong number."

I saw it three days in a row.

But I don't say that out loud.

"Becky," I say, "let me ask you this. I found it. Why do I have to pick it up?"

Becky says "Let me convene a meeting of the rest of the Coven. Relax, I'll bring you a dime."

But now I couldn't relax.

I text my friend Steve. He is a lawyer and a very, very smart guy. I type "Hey, if you have a short window, I have a legal question to ask you." Which isn't exactly the truth but he is never going to get back to me if I text him and say I want to ask him about a dime I almost found on the ground.

He texts me back "Now." Steve uses text as if the phone company is charging him by the word.

I call him and dispense with a preamble.

"You know how a found penny is supposed to bring you good luck?" There is no way I am going to mention dimes and dead people.

He now says "Seriously?" He also takes about ten seconds to pronounce the word. He and Becky should join a club. But I have him on the phone so I forge on. "Is the act of finding the penny enough or do you actually have to pocket the penny?"

167

"This is your legal question?"

"Well, it might be more a question of semantics."

"I don't know what you are asking."

"Do you have to pick up the penny and take it home or is the act of just spotting it enough to bring you luck?" I know I sound like an idiot. But I also know Steve is going to eventually get past the lunacy and give me his actual opinion. One I would never get from anyone else.

"You found a penny?"

"Say that I did."

"You didn't pick it up?"

"No."

"Why didn't you pick it up?"

"It doesn't matter. I just didn't."

"You understand that finding a penny does not bring you luck, right?"

"I do."

"Finding a million pennies on the other hand..."

"Steve. I'm just trying to settle an argument."

"I think you have to pick it up."

"I was afraid you were going to say that." And I am about to hang up when he says "Although." This word also takes about ten seconds to pronounce but this time I don't mind as much.

"Although what?" I ask.

"There is a dissenting opinion," he says.

"Go on," I say.

"I don't necessarily subscribe to it," he says.

"What?" I say.

"Full disclosure," he says, "it is from Rashi."

Rashi was a famed Jewish scholar and scribe.

"Bring it on," I reply.

"One could make the argument that leaving it on the ground is an act of kindness greater than the luck it bestows. Leaving the *mazel* for someone else is on a higher plane."

"I would be paying it forward."

"Your words not mine," he says.

I say "Ok thanks."

He says "You know how much I charge an hour for my opinion?"

"It is worth every cent," I reply. But he has already hung up.

I feel much better.

The minute I hang up from Steve, the phone rings again, it is Becky.

She says "I think since you woke me up you should buy me breakfast."

I say "Ok, I will meet you at Bagel Plus."

Becky and I have a great breakfast despite the group of unruly teenagers having coffee at the table beside us. Although I have driven and not gone on my daily walk, I am surprisingly famished. We share a mushroom omelette, egg white of course, and some lox bagel and cream cheese. Then I order French toast, which I know Becky will not touch.

"Look who has made a speedy recovery," she chides. "I was worried about you."

I say "Sorry about that. Just kinda lost my mind for a second."

I pay the bill and Becky and I get up to go. At the table next to us, the teenagers have left their waitress forty cents. I smile to myself and decide not to judge.

I hold the door open for Becky then say "Hold on, I'll be right back." I grab the four dimes and replace them with a toonie. When I get back outside I casually drop the coins at my feet.

Just in case someone needed a little Rashi backup.

THEO AND ME

My friend David calls and asks if I can do him a favor. I say it would be my pleasure. Although it most certainly will not. But it is what it is. He asks if I would agree to meet with his friend Theo. I tell him what I always tell him - that his friend Theo is a nut job.

"He's trying to get his book published," says David gently. "I told him you would help."

"He kinda freaks me out," I say. "What's with the beard?"

"His heart is in the right place," says David. Then, buttering me up he says "I told him nobody knows more about publishing than you."

"This makes us even?" I ask. David insists I once borrowed chairs from him for a party I did not invite him to.

David says "Not even close."

It was worth a try.

I agree to meet Theo at the Starbucks on Avenue near my house. I see him right away. He has nabbed a primo table near the bay window. I have begged him not to wear his tuxedo and top hat and he has met me halfway. He is in a brown wool three-piece suit and is wearing a fedora. He stands to greet me when I approach the table and extends a formal handshake.

"Hey Teddy," I say. "What's shaking?" I imagine he doesn't like being called Teddy but he has come calling, fedora in hand, and understands this is no time to put on airs.

"I am well," he says.

"Can I get you a coffee?"

"A mint tea," he replies, "and perhaps a thin slice of *sachertorte*." I don't tell him that Starbucks does not carry the Viennese chocolate cake first made for Prince Metterninch in 1832.

I bring him back his tea and a chocolate brownie.

"They ran out of the *sachertorte*," I say.

"Well, it is not surprising. It is 4:00 in the afternoon." Theo had wanted to meet at 7:00am.

"So what news with the book Theo?" I ask. I want to get this favor done sooner rather than later.

Theo pulls a letter out of his briefcase and waves it at me. "Those cretins at Random House have rejected my manuscript. They sent me a form letter, the anti-Semites!"

I take the letter from his hand. It is indeed a template rejection letter. 'We regret to inform you' etc.

"Look Theo," I say, reverting back to his given name in order not to pour salt on an open wound. "It is like I told you last time. You are wasting your time with the big publishers. They won't even consider a manuscript if it doesn't come from an agent."

Theo snatches the letter back "An agent," he scoffs. "I don't need no blasted agent. I have a glowing recommendation from Sokolov. A letter of introduction from the Baron himself!"

"Why don't you try the smaller presses?" I say. "I might know an editor at Summerled Press."

Theo calms down a little "Summerled? They do political manifestos?"

"Well, mostly poetry collections," I reply. "But they are looking to branch out."

The Summerled Press offices are in a Victorian in the Annex. Theo and I take an Uber because parking is a bitch in the Annex.

I do not know an editor at Summerled Press. I know the owner, Janet Summerled. She had gone out with my friend Harold Goldfarb. It had ended badly. Mostly for Goldfarb.

But I know her. We had broken bread half a dozen times. It was enough to get a meeting.

Theo cannot be talked out of his tuxedo and top hat this time. "You have to show people how serious you are." He lectures me in the Uber. I don't bother arguing with him. I had already used up all of my energy convincing him to allow me to get a copy translated from German into English.

Janet Summerled meets us in the Summerled Press conference room with two junior editors who I think are both called Maxine.

The meeting gets off to a good start.

If Janet and the two Maxines are surprised to be meeting a tall fully bearded man in tuxedo and tails then they are doing a remarkable job of disguising it.

And Theo, displaying both class and diplomacy, helps himself to the offered Timbits without once asking if he can have strudel instead.

Then Janet Summerled shocks me by saying "Theo, can I call you Theo, we are very interested in your book. We find it very compelling and are interested in publishing it."

Theo sits very straight in his chair and nods his head ever so slightly. As if to say, yes of course you are interested in publishing my book. Why wouldn't you. But I can tell he is pleased as punch.

"Yes," says one of the Maxines. "We really loved it."

"We did," says the other Maxine, "but we have notes."

"Notes?" I say. Although it might be a little muffled because I have a mouth full of Timbits.

"Notes?" Says Theo. "Vas is das?"

"Yes," says Janet Summerled. "To begin with. The title. I'm afraid it is a little on the nose."

"On the nose?" I say.

"On the nose?" Says Theo.

"Yes," replies one of the Maxines. "In this climate, we are trying to be a little more inclusive."

"That's right," pipes in the other Maxine. "Also we would like it to appeal to a broader audience. Let the people think that the state is for anyone and everyone."

Neither Theo or I say anything, although it looks like Theo is about to have a stroke. One of the Maxines takes our collective silence as a sign to soldier on.

"We like Teddy the Dreamer. Our creative team even mocked up a cover." She holds up a photo with the title and an illustration of Theo floating in the clouds. It is quite artistic.

"Yes," says Janet Summerled. "I do like that one. It's kinda catchy."

"The title is the title!" Theo says with a roar.

"Theo," I whisper, my mouth now Timbit free. "Let's be reasonable here. They want to publish your book."

"This is the name of the book," he repeats emphatically.

"Maybe you can make a little compromise?" I ask.

"There will be no compromise," says Theo. "This is not just a book. It is the future of my people. The name cannot be changed."

"That's a deal breaker," says Janet Summerled.

"Big time," says one of the Maxines.

All things considered, Theo is in a surprisingly good mood during the Uber ride home. He is the quintessential renaissance man. Schooled and learned in many disciplines. But, at the end of the day, he is a writer. And as a writer, he is buoyed by the fact that, despite their notes, they had liked his book.

"We shall publish it ourselves," he declares. "Like you do with your little joke books." I had suggested he self-publish when I first met him but this is no time for 'I told you sos'.

"You know how to do this?" Asks Theo. And actually, I do. I have an entire team set up to publish my own books on Amazon.

I say "Yes. I can do it for you. It is very easy."

"I can keep the name?" Says Theo.

"Yes," I assure him, "you keep the name."

He is very pleased.

"I am going to publish my book," he announces to our Uber driver.

Our driver, the confirmation email had said his name was Fernando, looks back and flashes a toothy smile. "Congratulations sir. I have a cousin back home in my country who published a book. It is a mystery novel."

"Fernando, where are you from?" I ask.

"Uganda," he replies.

"Ah," I say. "What is it like?"

"It is a beautiful country. But very, very hot."

"What do you think Theo? You want to go visit Uganda one day?"

Theo is busy shuffling the pages of his manuscript. He briefly looks up to say "Not for me, I don't do well in the heat."

Once my team gets the green light, things move along very quickly. Marianne sets up an Amazon account, Tatiana goes to work on the cover, and Helen does the design for the Kindle eBook and paperback. We use the Sokolov and Baron de Rothchild blurbs on the back cover. Miles sends out advance copies and we get surprisingly good reviews in both Kirkus ("a tour de force") and Publisher's Weekly ("his vivid imagination is matched only by his explosive use of language").

Theo wants to buy a new suit for the picture we plan on using for the author's page. I tell him I will take him to Yorkdale on Wednesday afternoon.

"Afternoon?" He asks.

"Yes," I reply. "Maybe around three."

"I prefer the morning," he says.

"In the morning," I reply, "I have to go to court."

"You have to go to court," he exclaims. "You have a trial?"

"Not so much a trial," I say. "I am fighting a speeding ticket." Theo says he will go to court with me then we will go to Yorkdale to buy a suit.

I have no case. I was really only hoping the cop wouldn't show but he did. The judge fines me $400 for going 30 km over the speed limit and dings me 2 points.

"Fucking injustice," I say to Theo speaking through the curtain as he tries on a suit in the change room at The Bay. "So fucking unfair."

Theo comes out of the change room wearing a brown three-piece suit which looks remarkably like the one he already owns. He gives me a twirl and then says:

"You were speeding my good man. Give it a rest."

David and Leanne have a book launch party. Leanne has even learned how to make *sachertorte*. It is a pretty big crowd. Even Lewberg and Goldfarb come.

David has set Theo up with a little table and there is a long line of people waiting for autographs.

Then Theo, who is in his customary tuxedo and top hat, stands up and raises his glass.

"I would like to thank David and Leanne for this beautiful party and my friend Ron for helping me realize my lifelong dream."

Everyone says "Hear hear."

And then I say "Theo, if you will it, it is not a dream."

And Theo smiles and says, "So corny. Maybe you should leave the writing to me."

I smile and said "Ok." I pick up the book and admire the cover. Tatiana did a good job -

"The Judenstadt by Theodor Herzl."

Then I help myself to my third piece of *sachertorte*.

AIN'T NO SUNSHINE

Photograph © Andrea Piacquadio / 123rf.com

Whenever I say "Did I ever tell you the story about the time I got punched in the face," some smart aleck will invariably say something like "I can't believe it only happened once," or "You must have a lot of stories to choose from". This usually gets a big laugh and I often have to wait for the laughter to subside before I can launch into the story. It's ok, I can give as good as I get.

I used to tell the story almost every time I heard the Bill Withers song Ain't No Sunshine. The song would start and I would say "Did I ever tell you the story about the time I got punched in the face?" Then someone would say - well, you get the picture.

It is a pretty good story and I have told it quite often because it turns out Ain't No Sunshine gets played a lot more than you would think. Especially if, like me, you have your car radio set to the Sirius station The Bridge, which plays acoustic rock all the time. Anyway, my friends and family have heard the story more times than they would care to and have sort of sucked the life out of it. Which, I guess, is fair enough but it has gotten to the point that when the song comes on my sister-in-law will, without looking up from her book, say "And then blah blah blah, I got punched in the face." Which also usually gets a good laugh.

So I don't tell it that much anymore and, if I do, I resort to the very condensed version which leaves out a lot of context and also, and this is the part I am not that crazy about, makes me look like a bit of a dick who deserved to get punched in the face.

Claire and I were on a double date with her friend Margaret and this guy Max she knew from the office. It was a set up. Claire had told me not to talk about stamps, coins, or birdwatching. She had told me to just try to get along. We were at a booth at the Rex, waiting for the band, a jazz trio, to come on. Music was blaring from the speakers. Bill Withers' Ain't No Sunshine came on. I didn't launch into my story about the time I got punched in the face because at that point I had not yet been punched in the face. But I was about to.

Max turned to Margaret and said "Little known fact. Bill Withers says 'I know' 22 times in the song. One of the all-time great trivia questions."
Margaret said "'Really?"
Max said "Yeah really."
And I thought to myself. Not so much.

Now I don't know if Claire tells this story. She has a new boyfriend and I am sure she has better things to talk about than the time her ex-boyfriend got punched in the face. Things didn't end up great with us so there is a chance that when she hears the song a smile might unfurl on her face. I'm not saying that makes her a bad person. I mean, it is probably just Pavlovian. But, if you ask her she will probably tell you that what happened next happened because I was a bit jealous. Which might be true. I should probably have mentioned that Max was Claire's ex-boyfriend. Just before me. He didn't collect stamps. He collected vintage Corvettes.

Now Max was right about the fact that the number of times Bill Withers says 'I know' in Ain't No Sunshine was a good trivia question. Not one of the all-time great trivia questions. But a good one.
What he wasn't right about was the number of 'I knows'.
It was not 22.
It was 26.
So I said "It isn't 22. It's 26."
And he said "No, it's 22."
And I said "26."
And he said "22."
And I said "Let's go ask the bartender to play the song again. Then we can count."
So together we got up and went to the bar in order to ask the bartender to play the song again.

If I write this story up, all good and proper-like, there is a chance I will scan up and read what I have just written and maybe think to myself exactly what you might be thinking to yourself right now.

22 or 26. What difference does it make? I was being petty and picayune. I was the type of guy who said picayune. Maybe you're thinking the kind of guy who says picayune probably deserves to get punched in the face.

In our rush to get to the bar, Max bumped into a guy carrying a pitcher of beer. The guy spilled half the beer. Words were exchanged. I won't mention the words. My friend Brian's father Irv says I say fuck too much. But you can probably guess. The guy then calmly put the pitcher down and then took a swing at Max. Max ducked.

And I got hit square in the face.

Like I said, this is the short version. I'm leaving out a lot of details. If I write it up all proper-like I will mention the fight Claire and I had in the car on the way to the bar. I will add a little color to illustrate the tension at the table. I'll explain that my friend Dani's husband Avi owns The Rex and he was working the bar that night which is why I knew I could get him to play the song again. Avi even gives me the backstory about the guy who hit me. Believe me, I can stretch it out. On the other hand, this isn't even close to being the shortest version. The next day, on my way to pick up my morning bagel, I walked by my neighbour who asked me how I got that shiner. That's what he said. "How'd you get that shiner?" He was old school. I didn't really want to chat so I said "Got hit by an errant fist". That's it. Six words. No mention of Bill Withers. This version is The Odyssey in comparison.

Of the three other people in this story, the only person I still speak to is Max. He lives down the street and I will run in to him at Starbucks from time to time. He's a pretty nice guy. He once even loaned me his Corvette. I finally had to tell him to stop apologizing for me getting punched in the face. I saw Margaret at United Bakers once and I waved to her. She didn't wave back.

Bill Withers died in March, 2020. He was 81. He wrote and recorded Ain't No Sunshine at the age of 31 for his debut album. Before becoming a musician, he was making toilets for airplanes. He was a working-class man who went on to write one of the greatest ballads of all time. When I listen to the song now I am always shocked to be reminded the song is only 2 minutes long. It seems so much bigger. He said the 'I knows' were originally going to be placeholders - that his intention was to write more lyrics, but the experienced musicians in the room, Graham Nash, Stephen Stills, and Booker T and the MGs, told him to keep them in. So he did. They became iconic. When I tell the story, I assume everyone knows the song. If you don't, stop reading and go listen to it. It is great. It is worth getting punched in the face for.

On the way home from The Rex, a bag of ice pressed on my face, Claire said "I should have said 'no stamps, no coins, no birdwatching and no Bill Withers.'" Which was pretty funny. Claire had a good sense of humor.

Then she said:

"You know it wouldn't have happened if you had just left it alone right?"

And I said "I know, I know."

Count 'em. 26.

HANONO

Photograph © Volodymyr Melnyk / 123rf.com

My friend Catherine is at my door. She lives three blocks away. She knows knocking on my door will get my attention faster than a phone call.

"Do you want to play poker tonight?"

I make a face. Catherine plays in a lot of games. I am not crazy about all of her people.

She has anticipated my reaction.

"This is a really good game," she says, countering whatever excuse I was about to make. "One of the partners at my firm, this guy Sami, has a regular home game. Stakes are decent. Really nice guys. Very laid back. Everyone plays well. And he has great desserts."

I have no plans. I have already eaten my frozen pizza. I could really go for some good dessert. I say "Ok."

She says "Come now. Mitchell is already in the car." She knows better than to give me time to change my mind.

I say "Fine. Let me just go pee."

The first thing Mitchell says when I get in the car is "Did Catherine tell you?" Now this could mean a lot of things. Catherine likes to operate on a need to know basis.

Catherine says "I didn't even need to." Turning to me she says "I had a proverbial ace up my sleeve."

I say "You know, you use proverbial way too much. What is your ace?"

"They are Egyptians," she says, knowing my parents were from Egypt. "It is an Egyptian poker game!"

"Really? I used to love playing poker with Egyptians."

And Catherine says to Mitchell "See! I told you he would like it."

An Egyptian poker game. It will give me the chance to use my Arabic.

Now, I don't speak Arabic.

Although my parents were born in Egypt and spoke it fluently, we spoke mainly French and then English in the house. But I used to play in a poker game at the Hemispheres condo building in Hallandale with my late Uncle Henri and his crew of octogenarian Egyptians. So, while I did not know how to speak Arabic, I could play poker in Arabic. I had picked up about two dozen words and expressions.

And I was determined to use one of them.

In truth, the actual poker was played mostly in French with a smattering of English. The cards, neuf de pique, valet de carreaux, were all described in French. The poker hands were a little more polyglot. A full house was a full, although pronounced much like the fava bean dish which was a staple of Egyptian life. A flush was a flush. But a straight was a quinte, which is French, while the rare straight flush, was a quinte flush, a French/English hybrid. Finally, a really lousy hand earned the Arabic designation of 'khara' - just shit. If the actual poker terminology was a little pedestrian, the banter and trash-talk were anything but.

Most of the men in this group had played together since they were teenagers. Their insults, in Arabic and French, had not changed. Which meant they were, by and large, juvenile and puerile. But, with age and maturity came the addition of Arabic idioms and expressions. Some of them were beauties.

I had some favorites. When someone had no clue what they were doing, invariably it was the hapless but loveable Edward Shweck, my uncle Andre would say "Al atrash fil alzifa." Which literally means 'like a deaf man at a wedding'.

Raymond Ben-Simon had the reputation of almost never playing a hand unless he had great cards. So he folded almost all of the time. On those rare occasions when he finally played a hand but lost, Tico was ready with his taunt.

"Sam Sam Sam ou fitir àla bassala."

He fasted fasted fasted and had breakfast with an onion.

Sometimes, the introduction of one idiom would bring a rash of others; seemingly unrelated non-sequiturs.

When my Uncle Henri scooped a pot after making a big bet which went unchallenged, he would wag his finger at me, often I wasn't even in the hand, and say:

"El hekaya labsa melaya."

Literally it means the story is wearing a bedsheet. It is used to say there's more to it than it seems. More to the story than meets the eye.

El hekaya labsa melaya.

I love that. Would make for a great book title.

It would be repeated with nodding heads and wry smiles. They looked a lot like our poker group does when we reminisce about the 1981 Springsteen concert.

There were others, but my all-time favorite was not an idiom. It was a single word. It was usually used, or at least instigated, by my uncle Henri and most often directed at his childhood friend Tico. Tico, may he rest in peace, was a very conservative player and generally took a long time to throw a chip in the pot. My uncle Henri would berate him by saying "Tico, ne sois pas hanono." Tico, don't be cheap. The French sentence with the Arabic last word which was our family trademark.

Hanono.

It was a great word. In a sentence or as a stand-alone. Hanono. I never said it. I never had the guts. It was not my place. Not with this group. I would have loved to have used it in some of my games in Toronto - there was no lack of deserving recipients - but nobody there spoke Arabic. But tonight, I would be playing poker with Egyptians. Now, I am not foolish enough to direct it at complete strangers. Catherine and Mitchell, on the other hand, though truthfully the furthest thing from cheap, are fair game. I just need to find the right moment. I just need one of them to make a bad fold.

Catherine was right. Sami and his three friends, all Egyptians, are really nice and very good poker players to boot. The stakes are reasonable but just large enough to have to make decisions, and everyone plays well and quickly. Along with Sami, there is

Sayed, Maurice, and Whalid. Sami is the Uncle Henri of the group. Clearly the leader, he is prone to making big bluffs and even bigger insults. Sayed is the conservative mild-mannered Raymond Ben-Simon. He mostly folds and nervously eats sunflower seeds. I don't think anyone could be Tico but Whalid comes a little close. He has a cloud over his head, loses a bunch of close hands, and is generally the brunt of most of the jokes. Mostly, they call him 'humar', which is donkey. He seethes when he loses a hand and Sami uses an expression I had heard with my own Egyptian group.

"Fokak men nafsak."

Unscrew yourself from yourself.

In other words, take it easy. Sami explains it to the table. "That is a great expression," says Mitchell. Catherine glares at me and I glare back. I am waiting to use my own great expression. But the cards are not helping.

An hour goes by and Catherine and Mitchell have barely folded a hand. Catherine is actually raking in most of the pots and Mitchell is holding his own. I have had plenty of opportunity to throw in a 'mabruk' (congratulations) after a won pot or a 'moosh raali' (not expensive) after calling a bet, or an 'abadan' (I have nothing), when caught in a bluff, but no, I have abstained. I am locked in to 'hanono'.

By hour two, I am getting a little desperate. When the moment comes, it does not even rise to the level of anything. It is just a fold. There is a small raise and everyone calls except for Catherine, who folds and a second later asks "Where is the restroom?" But between the time she said "fold" and the time she said "Where is the restroom?" I managed to triumphantly shout out "hanono!"

Everyone looks at me. Each with a quizzical look on their face. So I say it again: "hanono."

Catherine says "What does that mean?"

And I reply "It means cheap in Arabic."

And Sami says "I don't think it does."

And I say, to the four Egyptians "Yes it does." And, thinking maybe my pronunciation was off, repeat it again slowly: "ha-no-no".

Sayed, who is a pediatrician says "I don't think that is a word in Arabic." He says it in a very kind and gentle manner, like he is speaking to one of his patients.

I say "My family is from Cairo. From Heliopolis. I used to hear it all the time."

Sayed says "I am also from Heliopolis. But I have never heard that word."

And Sami says "I'm sorry. In Arabic cheap is 'Rakhis'. There are a few other adjectives and colloquialisms. But I have never heard of hanono. Sorry."

I say "Oh. I'm sorry."

And Catherine says "I'm not cheap, I just had to go to the bathroom."

The table falls quiet.

Sami says maybe this would be a good time to have dessert.

Again, Catherine was right. The desserts are delicious. They had been made by Sami himself, apparently the chef in the family. The table has pistachio and honey-laden Konafa, basbousa, which is semolina cake soaked in syrup, and zalabya, the fried balls of dough which my cousins and I knew would be waiting for us every time we visited our Tante Racheline. Were it not for the hanono debacle I would tell Sami and Sayed, the Heliopolis native, that dessert is almost as good as the pastries at Om Met Kek on Rue Ismaili Pasha.

The game resumes without incident. It is still fun but the air has gone out of the room. In the car on the way home Catherine says "What was that all about?"

I say "I don't know."

She says "I thought you could speak some words in Arabic?"

And I say "So did I."

The next day, I call my Tante Odette.

"Comment ça va?" I ask.

As usual, she answers "Zay el zift, merci." I am shit, thank you.

"Dis moi, tell me. When Henri called Tico hanono. What did it mean?"

"Hanono? Hanono meant he was calling him cheap."

I say "In Arabic?"

Odette says "No."

"Not in Arabic?"

And Odette says "No."

"Is it French?" Although I know it isn't.

And Odette says "No."

I say "So what language is it?"

Odette says "What language? It isn't any language. It is his name."

"Whose name?" I ask.

She says "Marcel Hanono. He was at school with your father and uncle in Cairo. Il était très avars. He was very cheap."

Marcel Hanono. My all-time favorite Arabic word is not Arabic at all.

I say "Ok thanks."

She says "Yallah bye," and hangs up.

I sit in silence for a few seconds then scream out "Fuuuuuuck!!"

I just hope it isn't someone's name.

LOS PANTERAS BLANCAS

One of the things a lot of people don't know about me is that I am a member of a violent and criminal Dominican gang known as Los Panteras Blancas. The White Panthers. We refer to ourselves, as do our rival gangs, just as the Blancas. Which doesn't really make a whole lot of sense to me because if you have the word panther in your gang name you'd think you would want to make it front and center. But not us Blancas. The gang originated in the DR, which is what we gang members call the Dominican Republic, but now has branches in Los Angeles, Phoenix, and Miami. Probably other places too. I'm not exactly an official member. Because that would require a tattoo of a white panther on my chest, a blood oath, and participation in a drive by shooting. I'm more of what you would call an honorary member. Like, if it were a golf club, I could play the course a few times a year but not be allowed to sign for drinks at the bar. That kind of thing.

I was made a member by Hector Alvarez Ramirez. You might have read about him. He's in jail for... well, if you read about it you know what he is in jail for. But he's appealing the case so, as a gang member, I really should be operating under the cloak of omertà. Anyway, Hector, if you're reading this, Toronto says hi. That's what Hector calls me. Toronto.

Hector thinks I saved his son from drowning. But I did no such thing. Hector, I did no such thing. But Hector thinks I am being modest so I decided it was probably not a good idea to argue with the head of Los Panteras Blancas. If he wants to think I saved his son, who am I to argue.

What happened was I was playing the Cana Golf Club in Punta Cana. It is a beautiful course. Number five is a par 3 where the green actually juts into the sea. And, because of the ocean breezes, you have to aim into the ocean and hope the wind pushes your ball back onto the green. As a result, a lot, and I mean a lot, of balls go into the water. So much so there were usually a couple of kids in rowboats retrieving the balls then selling them back to the tourists - three for twenty bucks. Anyway, I aimed left and my caddy told me I wasn't aiming left enough. So I adjusted and plunked two balls right into the ocean. I had to figure the caddy was getting a cut from the kids but it was such a beautiful golf course and such a stunning hole, that I didn't really care. I gingerly walked down the embankment in order to buy my allotment of balls from the waif in the rowboat. When he got out of the boat, he slipped and fell into the water. To be clear, the water at that spot was barely knee high. I reached down and gave him a hand up. Which is when Hector Alvarez Ramirez arrived on a jet ski. Words were exchanged between the boy who, it turned out, was his son, Hector, and my caddy. Words in Spanish which I did not understand. I stood there hoping a triple bogey and two lost balls was the worse which was going to happen to me. Then Hector stuck out his hand and said "Gracias. You have saved my son from drowning."

And I said "Oh no. There must be some misunderstanding. I just gave him a hand up. I hit two balls in the water you see." Then I smiled.

This was followed by another flurry of words and sentences in Spanish. Some, sounding very animated.

Then Hector shook my hand again and said, "You have saved my son."

At this point I did not know who he was and had never heard of the Blancas. He did have a large tattoo of a white animal, which I now know is a panther, on his chest but I had no way of knowing it was a gang mark and not a result of a night of too much revelling. But, not being a fan of conflict at the best of times, and faced with what can only be described as burning rage emanating from his eyes, I decided my best course of action was just to say "De nada" and move on to the next hole without peeing down my golf shorts.

Which is what I started to do.

But Hector then grabbed my arm and asked me where I was from. I told him I was from Toronto.

He said "Toronto, you are now a Blanco. You are one of us. You are protected anywhere you go. You are a Blanco. You are my brother. Mi hermano."

I said, "Gracias." Then he hugged me and said, "Say you are my brother."

So I said, "You are my brother." I mean, I actually already have a brother but he doesn't have a tattoo and usually doesn't scare the shit out of me. Then I said "Adios" and went back to my golf cart.

When we got to number six, my caddy said, "Dio Madre. Do you know who that was?" Then he told me. As you can imagine, I had trouble hitting the ball after that and decided to quit after nine.

That was seven years ago. I never heard from Hector again. I have never been back to the Dominican Republic. I don't really know any other Blancas. It's not as if there is a newsletter or anything. As luck would have it, I don't really get into much gang related trouble in Boca and, truth be told, I had kinda forgotten all about it. I guess I liked having an insurance policy but was also glad I never had to use it. It was a little like an EpiPen. I was only reminded of it because Hector had been in the news. He was in jail in Miami. Because, well, you know.

Anyway, Lewberg, Goldfarb and I were going to the Capital Grill at the Boca Town Center. It was supposed to be just the three of us but Goldfarb begged us to let him bring his new girlfriend - Yolanda. We liked Yolanda. She was good for Goldfarb. She was good company. Only, she had a tendency to sometimes get a tiny bit hot under the collar. Goldfarb insisted on driving because Yolanda wanted to sit up front. Lewberg didn't care because he preferred not to drive and I, I didn't mind sitting in the back of Goldfarb's Crown Victoria, it had plenty of room, and it meant I could leave my driving glasses at home, but I knew Goldfarb would not only not valet but he would circle round and round in order to get the best possible spot. Which is what happened. This usually drove me crazy. But this time it was not so bad. He made one lap and then timed it perfectly just as a Mercedes pulled out of a spot right in front of the restaurant. He drove past the spot, as one does in order to back in and just as he began to back up, as you might have guessed, a car behind us made a screeching turn, swooped in and took the spot. Now Lewberg, Goldfarb and I are always perfectly happy to let people steal our spots. This was South Florida after all. You never knew who you could run into. And the Town Center had plenty of spots. But Yolanda was having none of it. She jumped out of the car and unleashed a torrent of insults in English and another language which I think may have been Romanian. The driver of the car, which was a pimped-out muscle car - a Trans Am I think, got out with a few insults of his own. I don't think any were in Romanian. He was tall and shirtless. His chest was covered in tattoos. The three of us got out in order to pull Yolanda back into the car.

He said, "You need to control your chica," then he flashed a gun. I don't know what kind of gun it was. But it looked big. But I wasn't really looking at his gun. I was looking at the tattoo of a white panther on his chest.

Then, summoning courage I did not have, I said:

"I like your tat amigo."

And he said "Yeah. Thanks."

"I have a friend with the same tat. Hector. You know my friend Hector?"

And he said "Hector? I don't think so man."

And I said, "I think you do. My friend Hector says it's not polite to steal a brother's parking spot. Because," and I now pounded my chest and its non-existent tattoo, "I am your brother man. You hear me. I am your brother and you are my brother."

And he shrugged his shoulders and said "Ok brother." Then he got into the Trans Am and pulled out of the spot. Goldfarb got into the Crown Vic and backed it in.

We then went into the Capital Grill and toasted my courage and manliness with their signature Stoli Dollies.

Lewberg said, "That was straight up gangsta."

I should have let the accolades rain down on me for a little longer but knew it wasn't fair. When the second round of drinks arrived, I came clean and told them all about the golf course in the DR, about Hector, and about being an honorary member of Los Panteras Blancas.

"Wholly shit!" said Yolanda. "You're a gang member?"

I said "I guess I am. Who would have thought I would find another member at the Boca Town Center? I couldn't believe it when I saw that tattoo. A white panther!"

Goldfarb said, "You might want to order another drink."

I said "Yup. Tonight is worth celebrating."

And Goldfarb said, "No, because that wasn't a panther you blind fuck, that was a dolphin!"

MY IMAGINARY GIRLFRIEND

Photograph © Gerd Altmann / pixabay

I had only seen one on television but when I opened the front door and walked into the house I knew immediately I had walked into an intervention.

Doctors will tell you if you hear hooves you should think horse and not zebra so even though my birthday was six months away, I still should have figured surprise party - horse, and not intervention - zebra, but I knew right away it was an intervention.

Besides, sometimes it's just going to be a zebra.

So instead of 'Happy birthday,' someone loudly whispered "He's here," and there was nervous shuffling in the living room.

It was a pretty good crew. My brother and sister-in-law, my nieces, their husbands and boyfriends, even Jake the Snake had come in from Vancouver. Allie and Cory were there too. Everyone had a copy of *Not Book Club Material*. Except for Cory who was holding a guitar.

It would have been a good crew for a birthday party.

But it wasn't a party.

It was an intervention.

I wasn't surprised to see that Sammy was leading the intervention. She is a clinical psychologist. She spoke first.

"Uncle Ronnie," she said in her calming professional voice, "you first have to know that everyone in this room loves you."

Oh boy.

"And it is important you understand we only have your best interest at heart. We don't care who you date. We are only concerned when you keep it a secret."

Now I understood.

It was about Claire.

Sammy confirmed it. "It's about Claire," she said.

One of the perks of being a writer is it has allowed me to construct the illusion of a robust and active, albeit dysfunctional, social life. My stories are peppered with references to dates, girlfriends and paramours. And while it is true that some of these liaisons are real, although disguised and distorted, the majority are spun out of whole cloth, and built up primarily in order to have them fall - thereby giving the reader a ring side seat to their demise.

A girlfriend is introduced of course not as a way to highlight my suspect virility or heretofore unexplained attractiveness, but rather, as a way to add conflict. Because, with conflict, comes humor. I can be a little heavy handed with it. Like the crushed chilies I add to my chicken cacciatore.

So I rack my brain and come up with names for each story; names which my friend Carainn says look like they have been plucked from a Catskills kosher singles weekend registry.

Aviva. Hannah. Miriam. Sarah.

I scatter them amidst my stories like the ashes of someone recently departed, making sure I don't repeat names or confuse them with characters who have appeared in other stories.

Except for Claire.

Claire is in three separate stories.

"There is no Claire," I said. "I made her up. She is imaginary."

"Why is she in three stories?" Asked Rena. She is the youngest but it's tough to get anything past her.

"I wanted to link the stories," I replied. Which was true; sometimes there is something to be said for recurring characters. "Besides," I continued defensively, "it's not easy to keep coming up with new names." Which was also true.

"Uncle Ronnie," chimed in Danna, "just admit you have a girlfriend and we will move on. It's not a big deal.

"Even if I did," I said, both getting my back up and operating under the 'best defense is a good offense' maxim, "and I'm not saying I do. If you had bothered to read the entire book you would know that Claire and I broke up. It's right there in *Ain't No Sunshine*."

"Hmm," said Rachel. "That break up is sketchy. Nobody here believes it's real."

"Well of course it's not real," I countered, "because there is nobody real to have broken up with!"

"Here's my theory Uncle Ronnie," said Samantha in a voice she might use to talk someone off a ledge. "You had three good stories which you just had to tell. But it meant you had to reveal your girlfriend. I just don't think it is a coincidence."

I turned to Allie, who is my best friend, and said "Can you please tell them there is no girlfriend."

Then Allie, with Cory strumming his guitar by her side, gently tossed me under the bus. "You almost never pick up the phone. I can't account for a lot of your hours."

Then Rachel said "Hah!"

I said "Believe me, I wish you were right. But there is no girlfriend."

And then Caroline said, "We don't care if she isn't Jewish. We just want you to be happy."

"Whoa," I said. "Who said Claire wasn't Jewish?"

"*Claire*, Uncle Ronnie?" Said Danna.

"Claire could be a Jewish name. I know a lot of Jewish Claires. Besides, that isn't even her real name."

"Aha," said Rachel.

"There is no Claire. She is made up. She is an imaginary girlfriend."

Then Cory stopped strumming the guitar and said "I think you doth protest too much."

This went on for about an hour. Everyone had a theory. I batted every one down but I'm not sure anyone believed me.

It turns out though that interventions, if you can put up with the badgering and endless questions, feature excellent spreads. Maybe even better than birthday party food.

Caroline had even bought two different types of ice cream cake.

So it wasn't all that bad.

All of this talk of Claire made me a little sad. She was my favorite of my imaginary girlfriends. I might have written her up a little cold, overly sensitive, and quick tempered but she was also sweet and caring and considerate. I went through the content of *Ain't No Sunshine* in my head to see if it offered any clues as to why we broke up but my usual sparse and non-descriptive prose had come back to haunt me. Hoisting me, as it were, on my own petard. The story implied she had left me and it was the only thing I could infer. Claire did not suffer fools gladly and perhaps I was the fool with whom she wanted to suffer with no more. Still though, I hadn't really done anything that bad. She had forgiven me for both my foray into birdwatching and my ill-advised Italo Svevo dinner invitation. At least, that's what she told me. Maybe she still had feelings for me.

I drove to her apartment. It was late but she let me in without a thought. When I walked in I found Claire playing chess with the Angel of Death. She was a good player. Much better than me but she had a tendency to bring her queen out too early. That was fine against me but the Angel of Death would see right through it. She was already down some material and I watched in silence as she debated her next move. She wisely retreated her queen.

She looked up at me and said:

"Hey Hon. Where have you been?"

Just like that. As if we hadn't even broken up three stories ago.

"Birthday party," I replied.

"Fun! How did it go?" She asked.

"Not bad," I replied. "Two different types of ice cream cake. I brought some back. Do you want a piece?"

"No thanks. I am stuffed," she replied. Then, looking up at the Angel of Death she said "Nu? Are you going to make a move or do I have to wait until Simcha Torah."

And that's the story of how I got back together with Claire.

Sometimes it pays to be a writer.

ABOUT THE AUTHOR

Aaron Zevy is a writer and publisher from Toronto, Canada. He is the author of *Almost the Truth: Stories and Lies* and *The Bubbe Meise and Other Stories*.

Not Book Club Material is his third story collection.